EXAM ESSENTIALS PRACTICE TESTS

Cambridge English: First (FCE)

1

Charles Osbourne
with new material by Helen Chilton
and Helen Tiliouine

NATIONAL GEOGRAPHIC LEARNING | CENGAGE Learning

Australia • Brazil • Japan • Korea • Mexico • Singapore • Spain • United Kingdom • United States

Exam Essentials Practice Tests 1
Cambridge English: First (FCE) (without key)

Charles Osbourne with some new material by
Helen Chilton and Helen Tiliouine

Publisher: Gavin McLean

Publishing Consultant: Karen Spiller

Editorial Project Manager: Stephanie Parker

Development Editor: Debra Emmett

Strategic Marketing Manager: Charlotte Ellis

Project Editor: Tom Relf

Manufacturing Buyer: Eyvett Davis

Cover design: Oliver Hutton

Compositor: Cenveo® Publisher Services

National Geographic Liaison: Wesley Della Volla

Audio: Martin Williamson,
    Prolingua Productions

DVD-ROM: Tom, Dick and Debbie Ltd

Contributing writer: Elaine Hodgson
    (video materials)

ISBN: 978-1-285-74494-0

National Geographic Learning
Cheriton House, North Way, Andover, Hampshire, SP10 5BE
United Kingdom

Cengage Learning is a leading provider of customized learning solutions with office locations around the globe, including Singapore, the United Kingdom, Australia, Mexico, Brazil and Japan. Locate your local office at: **international.cengage.com/region**

Cengage Learning products are represented in Canada by Nelson Education, Ltd.

Visit National Geographic Learning online at **ngl.cengage.com**

Visit our corporate website at **www.cengage.com**

Photos
The publisher would like to thank the following sources for permission to reproduce their copyright protected photographs:

159 t (Getty Images), 159 b (Waldteufel/Fotolia), 160 t (Andreu Dalmau/Epa/Corbis UK Ltd), 160 b (Redferns/Getty Images), 162 t (Shutterstock), 163 t (BE&W Agencja Fotograficzna Sp. z o.o./Alamy), 163 b (David Fischer/Getty Images), 165 t (Getty Images), 165 b (Shutterstock), 166 t (Transtock Inc./Alamy), 166 b (Motoring Picture Library/Alamy), 168 t (Getty Images), 168 b (Shutterstock), 169 t (Shutterstock), 169 b (Yuri Arcurs/Fotolia), 171 t (Shutterstock), 171 b (Getty Images), 172 t (Blend Images/Alamy), 172 b (Purestock/Alamy), 174 t (Mar Photographics/Alamy), 174 b (Andrew Rubtsov/Alamy), 175 t (Bilderbox/Fotolia), 175 b (Shutterstock), 177 t (Getty Images), 177 b (UpperCut Images/Alamy), 178 t (Frans Lemmens/Alamy), 178 b (Paul Weston/Alamy), 180 t (Shutterstock), 180 b (Arthur Tilley/Getty Images), 181 t (Christine Osborne Pictures /Alamy), 181 b (Alexandre Zveiger/Fotolia).

Text
The publishers would like to thank the following for permission to use copyright material:

Page 12: Adapted from 'Wrestling with demons' by Simon Hattenstone, *The Guardian*, 21 July 2003, Copyright Guardian News & Media Ltd 2003. Page 32: Adapted from 'How I came to envy the country mice' by Diana Athill, *The Guardian*, 17 December 2003, Copyright Guardian News & Media Ltd 2003. Page 34: Adapted from 'The Common Hand' by Carl Zimmer, http://ngm.nationalgeographic.com/2012/05/hands/zimmer-text. Page 52: Adapted from 'In Search of an Old Romantic' by John Walsh, First appeared in *The Independent*. © 2004. Copyright The Independent, reproduced with permission. Page 70: Adapted from 'Travel's Frenemy: Noise' by Daisann McLane, http://travel.nationalgeographic.com/travel/traveler-magazine/real-travel/noise/. Page 72: Adapted from 'Mountains in the Sea' by Gregory S. Stone, http://ngm.nationalgeographic.com/2012/09/seamounts/stone-text. Page 88: Adapted from 'Photo Research' by Jim Richardson, http://photography.nationalgeographic.com/photography/photo-tips/photo-research-richardson/#page=2. Page 106: Adapted from 'Miracle Above Manhattan' by Paul Goldberger, http://ngm.nationalgeographic.com/2011/04/ny-high-line/goldberger-text. Page 124: From *Mountains of the Mind* by Robert Macfarlane. Copyright © 2003 by Robert Macfarlane. Used by permission of Pantheon Books, a division of Random House, Inc. and Granta Publications. Page 142: Adapted from Barrington Irving, from http://www.nationalgeographic.com/explorers/bios/barrington-irving/, copyright © National Geographic.

Although every effort has been made to contact copyright holders before publication, this has not always been possible. If notified, the publisher will undertake to rectify any errors or omissions at the earliest opportunity. Note that the sample answer sheets in the Practice tests are not the updated official answer sheets provided by Cambridge as these were not available at the time of publication.

Printed in China by RR Donnelley
Print Number: 06   Print Year: 2018

Contents

CAMBRIDGE ENGLISH: First (FCE)

Paper 1: READING AND USE OF ENGLISH (1 hour 15 minutes)

Part	Task type and focus	Number of questions	Task format
1	**Multiple-choice cloze** Task focus: vocabulary	8	A multiple-choice cloze text with eight gaps, followed by eight four-option questions.
2	**Open cloze** Task focus: grammar and some vocabulary	8	A modified cloze text with eight gaps which you must fill with the appropriate word.
3	**Word formation** Task focus: vocabulary	8	A text with eight gaps. You are asked to complete the text by making an appropriate word from the word prompt you are given for each gap.
4	**Key word transformations** Task focus: grammar and vocabulary	6	This task consists of six discrete key word transformations. You are asked to complete a sentence which means the same as the given sentence using the key word.
5	**Multiple choice** Task focus: reading for detailed understanding of a text, gist, opinion, attitude, tone, purpose, main idea, meaning from context, implication, text organisation features	6	You answer six four-option multiple-choice questions on a text.
6	**Gapped text** Task focus: reading to understand how a text is structured	6	Six sentences have been removed and placed in jumbled order after a text. You decide from where in the text the sentences have been removed.
7	**Multiple matching** Task focus: reading for specific information in a text, detail, opinion, attitude	10	You match ten questions with different texts or different sections of a text.

Paper 2: WRITING (1 hour 20 minutes)

Part	Task type and focus	Number of questions	Task format
1	**Question 1** Essay	Part 1 is compulsory. 140–190 words	You must write an essay based on a given title and accompanying ideas, including one of your own.
2	**(FIRST candidates)** **Questions 2–4** may include an article, an email/a letter, a report, a review.	You choose one task from a choice of three. 140–190 words	You must carry out a writing task, using the appropriate style and format.
2	**(FIRST FOR SCHOOLS candidates)** **Questions 2–4** may include an article, an email/a letter, a review, a story. **Question 5** is based on the set books. It may be an essay.	You choose one task from a choice of four. 140–190 words	You must carry out a writing task, using the appropriate style and format.

Paper 3: LISTENING (40 minutes approximately)

Part	Task type and focus	Number of questions	Task format
1	**Multiple choice** Task focus: understanding gist, detail, function, purpose, feeling, attitude, opinion, genre, agreement, etc.	8	A series of short unrelated extracts of approximately 30 seconds each, from monologues or exchanges between interacting speakers. There is one three-option question for each extract.
2	**Sentence completion** Task focus: detail, specific information, stated opinion	10	A monologue of 3–4 minutes. The task consists of ten gapped sentences.
3	**Multiple matching** Task focus: understanding gist, detail, function, purpose, feeling, attitude, opinion, genre, agreement, etc.	5	A series of short related extracts, of approximately 30 seconds each, from monologues. The five questions require selection of the correct option from a list of eight.
4	**Multiple choice** Task focus: understanding attitude and opinion, main idea, specific information and gist	7	A text between two speakers of 3–4 minutes. There are seven three-option questions.

Paper 4: SPEAKING (14 minutes approximately)

Part	Task format	Input	Functions
1 **Interview** 2 mins	The interlocutor asks each candidate to say a little about themselves.	Verbal questions	You must be able to • give personal information. • talk about present circumstances / past experiences. • talk about future plans.
2 **Individual long turn** 4 mins	Each candidate talks about a pair of photographs for 1 minute, followed by a 30-second response from the second candidate.	Visual stimuli, with verbal and written instructions	You must be able to • give information. • express your opinions. • relate photos to yourself and your own experience.
3 **Two-way collaborative task** 4 mins	The interlocutor asks candidates to carry out a task based on written prompts.	A written question with written stimuli and verbal instructions	You must be able to • exchange information and opinions. • express and justify opinions. • agree, disagree or partly agree. • suggest and speculate.
4 **Discussion** 4 mins	The interlocutor asks candidates general opinion questions related to the topic covered in Part 3.	Verbal prompts	You must be able to • exchange information and opinions. • express and justify opinions. • agree, disagree or partly agree.

Exam Essentials Practice Tests is a new series of materials published by National Geographic Learning for students preparing for the following major EFL/ESL examinations: Cambridge English: First (FCE), Cambridge English: Advanced (CAE), and Cambridge English: IELTS (International English Language Testing System). The series is characterised by the close attention each component pays to developing a detailed knowledge of the skills and strategies needed for success in each paper or part of the exams.

Cambridge English: First (FCE) Practice Tests helps learners become aware of the exam requirements for Cambridge English: First (FCE), offers details about the format and language in the exam, and helps learners develop exam skills necessary for success. The book also offers extensive practice in all parts of the exam, using the actual test format.

Taking the exam

Cambridge English: First is one of a series of five Cambridge English exams corresponding to different levels of the Common European Framework of Reference for Languages (CEFR):

• Cambridge English: Key (KET) CEFR Level A2

• Cambridge English: Preliminary (PET) CEFR Level B1

• Cambridge English: First (FCE) CEFR Level B2

• Cambridge English: Advanced (CAE) CEFR Level C1

• Cambridge English: Proficiency (CPE) CEFR Level C2

Cambridge English: First is widely recognised in commerce and industry, and by universities and similar educational institutions, as proof that the holder of this qualification can do office work or take a course of study in English.

The exam can be taken on many dates during a year, and can be taken on paper or on a computer. It consists of four Papers:

Paper 1, Reading and Use of English (1 hour 15 minutes)

Seven parts: four Use of English tasks including cloze tests, word formation and key word transformations focusing on vocabulary and grammar, followed by three reading comprehension tasks. The reading tasks consist of a long text followed by multiple-choice questions, a gapped text with whole sentences removed and a multiple-matching task. The focus in the reading tasks is on understanding gist, main points, detail, attitude, implication, purpose, opinion and text structure as well as deducing the meaning of words and phrases from context.

Paper 2, Writing (1 hour 20 minutes)

Two parts, each requiring you to produce a piece of writing. In Part 1, candidates of both Cambridge English: First and Cambridge English: First for Schools have to write a compulsory essay *in Part 1.*

In Part 2, 'Cambridge English: First' candidates choose one task from a choice of three questions. These may be an informal letter or email, a formal letter or email, an article, a report, or a review written for a given purpose and target reader.

In Part 2, 'Cambridge English: First for Schools' candidates choose one task from a choice of four questions. These may be an informal letter or email, an article, a review, a story, or a question on a set text written for a given purpose and target reader.

Paper 3, Listening (40 minutes approximately)

Four parts with recorded texts and comprehension questions. Tasks include multiple choice, sentence completion and multiple matching. The focus is on understanding gist meaning, main points or specific information, detail, purpose, function, feeling, attitude, opinion, genre and agreement.

Paper 4, Speaking (14 minutes approximately)

Four parts, involving two candidates and two examiners (one examiner asks the questions and the other listens). The Speaking Paper focuses on the candidates' ability to use general interactional and social language, organise a larger unit of discourse (comparing, describing, expressing opinions), sustain an interaction, exchange ideas, express and justify opinions, etc.

Preparing for the exam

In preparing for the four papers, the following points should be taken into account:

Reading and Use of English: To prepare for the **Use of English** (Parts 1, 2, 3 and 4), as well as getting general practice in grammar and vocabulary, you should practise the precise skills necessary for the tasks here: how to use a word or phrase in context, how words with similar meanings are used in different collocations, accuracy with common structures, phrasal verbs and lexical phrases, and the different methods of word formation.

To prepare for the **Reading** (Parts 5, 6 and 7) you need to be familiar with a range of reading materials, such as newspaper articles, advertisements, brochures, guides, manuals and correspondence, as well as with different approaches to reading. It is important be aware that different strategies can be used for different parts of the Reading

Paper. For example, reading to find specific information is the best strategy in Part 7, where candidates have to find out where a certain piece of information is located.

Writing: You must be able to write an essay for Part 1 and an article, email/a letter, essay, report, review, or story for Part 2 (see above for the difference between the content of Cambridge English: First and Cambridge English: First for Schools exams), so practice of these types of writing is essential. You should practise covering all the points provided in the input and your writing must display organisation and coherence, clear layout, appropriate register, control and accuracy of language.

Listening: Practice with pre-listening tasks (focusing on developing an expectation of what might be said) is essential here, as is thorough familiarity with a wide variety of spoken English in terms of discourse types and genres. Listening for different purposes should also be exercised: to get the gist or to find specific information.

Speaking: You need practice in using spoken English effectively, which includes mastery of conversational skills (such as turn taking and the appropriate way to participate in a discussion), providing full but natural answers to questions, requesting clarification and speaking clearly and audibly at all times.

Further information can be obtained from the following website: www.cambridgeenglish.org.

Practice Tests: contents

Cambridge English: First (FCE) in the *Exam Essentials Practice Tests* series prepares candidates for the Cambridge English: First examination by providing **eight full practice tests,** accurately following the latest exam specifications.

There are **two guided tests** at the beginning, which feature **essential tips** to practise exam strategy. These essential tips offer guidance and general strategies for approaching each task. Other tips offer advice relevant to specific questions in the guided tests. These two comprehensive guided tests will help students prepare for each paper in the ways described in the previous section, while the following **six tests (without guidance)** will offer students thorough practice up to and beyond the level of the exam.

The DVD-ROM accompanying the book includes the **audio materials** for Paper 3 (Listening), which have been recorded so as to accurately reflect the audio element of the actual exam. (Please see the DVD-ROM Introduction for more information about the content of this component.)

A **writing bank** includes sample answers for the tasks in Paper 2 (Writing), writing tips in the form of **notes**, and **useful phrases** and **expressions** for the different task types.

Varied **visual materials** for Paper 4 (Speaking) have also been included, while a **language bank** supplies useful phrases and expressions for use in the Speaking Paper when discussing the visual and written stimuli.

There is also a **glossary** at the end of each test, explaining vocabulary from Paper 1 that is likely to be unfamiliar to students.

Clear and straightforward design simplifies use of the book. **Exam overview** tables ensure that key information is readily accessible, while a specially designed menu makes it easy to navigate through the different papers and parts of each practice test.

You will find sample exam answer sheets on pages 156–158 which you can photocopy and use to note down your answers. These will give you practice in using the answer sheets provided in the real exam.

For more practice, there is also an additional book of tests for this exam: *Exam Essentials Practice tests 2, Cambridge English: First (FCE)*.

Practice Tests: principles

In writing this book, three guiding principles have been observed:

Firstly, that it should be useful for teachers, and for students whether sitting the Cambridge English: First exam for the first time, or re-sitting the exam, and whether working alone or in a class. Students approaching the exam for the first time would be best advised to work through the book linearly, developing their skills and confidence; those re-sitting the exam can consult the overview tables to concentrate on particular areas for targeted revision. The **without key** edition can be used by students working in a class, while the **with key** edition provides a detailed **answer key** and all the **audio scripts**, ensuring that students working alone can benefit from active support while attempting these tests.

The second principle is that the questions should accurately reflect the whole range of questions found in the Cambridge English: First exam. Thus students obtain guidance concerning the general content and the best way of approaching the tasks from the questions themselves. Seeing the questions in this light – as instructions to the candidate from the examiner, rather than intimidating challenges – also helps students feel less daunted by the whole experience of sitting a major exam like this.

The third principle is that the texts used in the practice tests should not only be fully representative of those used in the exam but also varied and interesting. Everyone finds it easier to learn a skill if the subject matter is relevant to his or her lifestyle and interests. In choosing, editing and creating the texts here, we have done our utmost to ensure that the experience of working with this book is as stimulating and rewarding as possible.

PAPER 1 Reading and ▶ Part 1
      Use of English Part 2
PAPER 2 Writing   Part 3
                     Part 4
PAPER 3 Listening   Part 5
PAPER 4 Speaking   Part 6
                     Part 7

For questions **1–8**, read the text below and decide which answer (**A, B, C** or **D**) best fits each gap. There is an example at the beginning (**0**).

Mark your answers **on the separate answer sheet**.

Example:

0 **A** idea   **B** view   **C** thought   **D** decision

0	A	B	C	D
	A	<u>B</u>	C	D

Essential tips

▶ Read the title and the whole text to get the general meaning.

▶ Some of the questions will ask you to choose a word from a set of words with similar meanings.

▶ The word you need may be part of a collocation, an idiom, an expression or fixed phrase. You may need a preposition, which is part of a phrasal verb or a linker.

▶ If you are not sure which of the options fits best, say the sentence to yourself and use the one that sounds best.

▶ When you have finished, read the text again to make sure it makes sense.

Question 3: The gapped word is part of a fixed phrase. Which verb best completes the phrase *when it ... to*?

Question 6: Sisters, brothers, grandparents are all ... of your family.

Question 8: The gapped word is part of a fixed expression. Which verb best completes the phrase *... the best for somebody*?

Working parents

Reliable studies have shown that children of parents who both go out to work have no more problems than children with one parent staying at home. My personal (**0**) .... is that both parents should go out to work if they wish.

Some parents invest so much in a career that they cannot (**1**) .... to give it up. Others have to work because of economic (**2**) ....

There are several options when it (**3**) .... to choosing childcare from child minders to the kind neighbour (**4**) .... the street.

No (**5**) .... how good the childcare may be, some children protest if their parents aren't around. Babies become dependent on parents and close family (**6**) .... , so parents should make sure they allow (**7**) .... time to help their child settle in with their new carer.

Remember: if parents want to (**8**) .... the best for their children, it's not the quantity of time they spend with them, it's the quality that matters.

1	**A** bear	**B** decide	**C** hope	**D** expect
2	**A** reason	**B** duty	**C** necessity	**D** task
3	**A** refers	**B** concerns	**C** turns	**D** comes
4	**A** of	**B** opposite	**C** across	**D** next to
5	**A** way	**B** matter	**C** surprise	**D** exception
6	**A** people	**B** adults	**C** members	**D** grown-ups
7	**A** little	**B** no	**C** lots	**D** plenty of
8	**A** make	**B** give	**C** have	**D** do

PAPER 1	Reading and Use of English ▸	Part 1
		Part 2
PAPER 2	Writing	Part 3
		Part 4
PAPER 3	Listening	Part 5
PAPER 4	Speaking	Part 6
		Part 7

For questions **9–16**, read the text below and think of the word which best fits each gap. Use only **one** word in each gap. There is an example at the beginning (**0**).

Write your answers **IN CAPITAL LETTERS on the separate answer sheet.**

Example: **0** B E E N ☐☐☐☐☐☐☐☐☐☐☐☐☐☐☐☐

Daniela: Skateboard champion

I've always (**0**) .... an outdoors kind of girl, and (**9**) .... a kid, I'd get up to all sorts of stuff with my friends – climbing trees and messing about in the woods. As we got older, my friends started doing other things (**10**) .... shopping and listening to music, but I still loved being outside and needed a new challenge.

(**11**) .... was my brother who first got me (**12**) .... skateboarding. I'd seen him practising on his board hour after hour, and to (**13**) .... honest, I used to think it was uncool. But when he showed me some amazing tricks he could do one day, I had to give it a go.

I've got a competitive streak, so I watched loads of skateboarding clips online and got out on my board whenever I could – even (**14**) .... it was dark – in order to compete (**15**) .... my brother. It obviously paid (**16**) .... because I beat him in a competition last month!

Essential tips

▸ Read the whole text to get the general meaning.

▸ Decide what kind of word is needed (verb, pronoun, article, determiner, quantifier, etc.).

▸ Remember you can only use one word in each gap.

▸ You cannot use contracted forms (*I've, he's, they're, mustn't,* etc.) to fill in the gaps.

▸ Say the phrase or sentence to yourself and see which word sounds right in each gap.

▸ Read the text when you have finished and check that it makes sense.

Question 10: Look at the context. The missing word means 'for example', or 'such as'.

Question 12: This gap is part of a phrasal verb that means 'to become interested in' an activity.

Question 13: The missing word helps to complete a common expression. Which verb and form of the verb is needed?

PAPER 1	Reading and ▶	Part 1
	Use of English	Part 2
		Part 3
PAPER 2	Writing	Part 4
		Part 5
PAPER 3	Listening	Part 6
PAPER 4	Speaking	Part 7

For questions **17–24**, read the text below. Use the word given in capitals at the end of some of the lines to form a word that fits in the gap **in the same line**. There is an example at the beginning (**0**).

Write your answers **IN CAPITAL LETTERS on the separate answer sheet.**

Example: | 0 | O | B | S | E | R | V | A | T | I | O | N | | | | | | | | |

Essential tips

▶ Read the whole text to get the general meaning.

▶ Decide what type of word (noun, adjective, verb, etc.) you need for each gap.

▶ Look at the context carefully. The word may be negative or positive.

▶ You may need to add a prefix or suffix to the prompt word.

▶ If the word is a noun, check if you need the singular or plural form.

▶ You may need to make two changes to the word (add a prefix and a suffix, add two suffixes, etc.).

▶ Check the spelling of each word carefully.

Question 21: In this gap you are looking for a noun. Read the rest of the sentence. Should the noun be singular or plural?

Question 22: This word describes the noun (*site*), so it must be an adjective. How can you form an adjective from *idea*?

Question 23: In this gap you are looking for an adverb. How many changes do you need to make in order to form an adverb from *surprise*?

The London Eye

The London Eye, the giant (**0**) …….. wheel, is one of the most   **OBSERVE**
popular attractions in London. The wheel is one of the tallest
of its kind, at a (**17**) …….. of 135 metres. 1,700 tons of steel were   **HIGH**
used for its (**18**) …….. . People make special journeys to see the   **CONSTRUCT**
(**19**) …….. wheel. Fifteen thousand visitors can ride on the   **EXCITE**
Eye every day.

The architects, Julia Barfield and her husband David Marks,
won the competition to design a Millennium landmark. Their
design was the most (**20**) …….. of all the projects and the first   **IMAGINE**
(**21**) …….. of the wheel were made on their kitchen table in 1993.   **DRAW**
Julia found the (**22**) …….. site by drawing a circle round London   **IDEA**
and finding its centre.

Not (**23**) …….. , it took about three years to get the wheel built.   **SURPRISE**
In (**24**) …….. of their work, the couple were awarded the MBE,   **RECOGNISE**
a special honour that is given in the UK to someone who has
achieved something special.

PAPER 1	Reading and Use of English ▶	Part 1
		Part 2
PAPER 2	Writing	Part 3
		Part 4
PAPER 3	Listening	Part 5
		Part 6
PAPER 4	Speaking	Part 7

For questions **25–30**, complete the second sentence so that it has a similar meaning to the first sentence, using the word given. **Do not change the word given.** You must use between **two** and **five** words, including the word given. Here is an example (**0**).

Example:

0 I'll be very happy when I go on holiday.

FORWARD

I'm .... on holiday.

The gap can be filled by the words 'looking forward to going' so you write:

Example: | **0** | LOOKING FORWARD TO GOING |

Write only the missing words **IN CAPITAL LETTERS on the separate answer sheet.**

Essential tips

▶ You must use between two and five words in the gap. Contractions (*didn't, we're, it's,* etc.) count as two words.

▶ Check that you have used all the information from the first sentence, and that you haven't added any more information.

▶ Make sure you don't change the word given in any way.

▶ Decide what structure you need to use (passive voice, indirect speech, etc.) by looking at what comes before and after the gap.

▶ Remember to check your spelling carefully.

Question 28: What verb is used with *better* to mean 'should'? After it do we use the infinitive with or without *to*? Must this be positive or negative?

Question 29: Here you need to use the passive. Your prompt word is *been*. What tense do you need?

Question 30: *Unless* means 'if not', so what change do you need to make to one of the verbs in this conditional sentence?

25 Richard asked me how much I had paid for the theatre tickets.

COST

Richard wanted to .... the theatre tickets.

26 It wasn't a good idea for you to delete that file.

SHOULD

You .... that file.

27 The ferry couldn't sail because the weather was bad.

DUE

The ferry couldn't sail .... weather.

28 The teacher told us not to be late on Friday.

BETTER

'You .... late on Friday,' the teacher said.

29 There are Spanish and French translations of the book.

BEEN

The book .... into Spanish and French.

30 She will only phone if she gets lost.

UNLESS

She will .... lost.

PAPER 1 Reading and
Use of English ▶
PAPER 2 Writing
PAPER 3 Listening
PAPER 4 Speaking

Part 1
Part 2
Part 3
Part 4
Part 5
Part 6
Part 7

You are going to read an article about a wrestler who became an author. For questions **31–36**, choose the answer (**A**, **B**, **C** or **D**) which you think fits best according to the text.

Mark your answers **on the separate answer sheet**.

The wrestler who became an author

Pete Watson looks like the biggest, sweetest teddy bear you ever saw. It is only when he opens his mouth that you notice the missing front teeth. Watson is a three-time world champion wrestler turned author. He was adored by fans because he was different: while other wrestlers were supreme athletes, he was just a hulk who knew how to take a hit. You could throw as many chairs as you liked at Pete Watson, you could smack him repeatedly, but he wouldn't go down.

After two autobiographies and a series of children's stories, he has just written a brilliant first novel: a work of immense power and subtlety, likely to gain a wide readership. At its simplest, it is about a boy and his dad getting together after a lifetime apart, though there is far more to it than that. Was he inspired by anyone he knew? The father, he says, is based on guys he met on the road – wrestlers, friends of his, who appeared to be leading exciting lives, but deep down were pretty miserable.

line 11 Watson does not come from traditional wrestling stock. He grew up in Long Island, New York. His father was an athletics director with a PhD, his mother a physical education teacher with two master's degrees – one in literature, the other in Russian history. He was a big boy, bullied for his size. One day his neighbour had a go at him, and for the first time Watson realised he could use his weight and size instead of feeling awkward about it. It was a turning point.

At college, he did a degree in communication studies. Meanwhile, he was learning the ropes of professional wrestling. Did his parents try to dissuade him? 'No. They were just really insistent that I finished college. I am pretty sure they thought I'd get hurt and quit wrestling.' But he didn't.

He looks in remarkably good condition for someone who spent 20 years in the ring. His skin is smooth and firm; there are few visible scars. 'It's amazing what retirement can do for you. I looked really rough five years ago, and now I think I look a good deal younger,' he says. People are surprised by the softness of his handshake. 'Yeah, that's the wrestler's handshake,' he says.

Do you have to be a good actor to be a good wrestler? 'I used to really resent the acting label, but it *is* acting. When it's really good, when you're feeling it and letting that real emotion fly, it comes closer to being real.' What did his children think when they saw him getting hurt? 'Well, they used to think I never got hurt because that's what I told them. When they got old enough to realise I did, they stopped enjoying it. That was, in part, what led to my decision to get out.'

Nowadays, his time is dedicated to family and books – his next novel is about boy wrestlers living on the same block, and he is also writing more children's stories. He does not think this life is so different from wrestling. 'Wrestling is all about characters,' he says. 'So when my fans hear I've written a novel, I don't get the sense that they feel I've abandoned them.'

▸ Read the text first to get the general meaning. Don't worry about individual words that you don't know.

▸ The questions follow the same order as the relevant information in the text.

▸ Underline the key words in each question and in the four options.

▸ Look in the text for information that supports one of these options, but don't expect to find exactly the same words.

Question 31: Look at option A. It consists of two parts: he frequently lost and he was not aggressive. If an option consists of two parts, it is correct only if both parts are correct. For example, it is true that Pete was not aggressive, but as he didn't frequently lose, option A is not correct.

Question 33: This is a question about vocabulary. If you don't know the meaning of the words (in this case *stock*), you can answer the question by looking at the context. The sentences after *traditional wrestling stock* are about his parents' professions. What is the correct option?

Question 34: An option is correct only if you can find clear support for it in the text. For instance, option C claims that Pete's parents wanted him to stop wrestling. Can you find support for that in the text? For which of the four options can you find support in the text?

31 What impression do we get of Pete Watson's skills as a wrestler?

A He frequently lost because he was not very aggressive.
B He was too gentle and friendly to be a good wrestler.
C He was injured a lot because he didn't fight back.
D His speciality was letting his opponent hit him.

32 It is suggested that Watson's first novel

A is based on his own autobiography.
B will be popular with those who liked his autobiographies.
C will not only appeal to his fans.
D is not much more than a simple story.

33 What does 'traditional wrestling stock' in line 11 refer to?

A Watson's childhood
B Watson's family background
C Watson's educational background
D Watson's background in athletics

34 What did Watson's parents feel about his interest in wrestling?

A They were afraid he would get hurt.
B They insisted that he should have proper training at college.
C They wanted him to give up wrestling.
D They thought he would abandon the sport quite soon.

35 How does Watson regard the idea that wrestling is like acting?

A He resents the suggestion.
B He thinks wrestlers aren't good actors.
C He has come to accept it.
D He doesn't think wrestling can compare to acting.

36 Watson's present life is not so different from his past profession because

A his work is still connected with characters.
B he is writing about wrestling, his previous profession.
C his family are still more important than anything else.
D his fans still follow his career with interest.

For the Glossary see page 27 ▶

PAPER 1 Reading and ▶ Part 1
         Use of English   Part 2

PAPER 2 Writing   Part 3
                            Part 4
PAPER 3 Listening   Part 5

PAPER 4 Speaking   Part 6
                            Part 7

You are going to read an article about computer games. Six sentences have been removed from the article. Choose from the sentences **A–G** the one which fits each gap (**37–42**). There is one extra sentence which you do not need to use.

Mark your answers **on the separate answer sheet**.

Films and computer games

In just a few decades the gaming industry has become a lot bigger than the film business. In terms of turnover, what is rather grandly called 'interactive entertainment' makes twice as much money as Hollywood cinema. Which of course leaves people in the film business wondering if they can harvest any of this new income. Is there any way of making films more appealing to people who regularly like to play computer games?

Making a film out of a best-selling computer game can certainly guarantee a large audience. **37**   New games have stunning action sequences that rely on fantasy effects, and now films are being released with similar scenes. Gravity is discarded as heroes leap across huge gaps, while slow-motion techniques show bullets moving through the rippling air.

A major segment of the gaming market comprises science-fiction games, and film-makers have started to realise that they could set films in similar sci-fi future worlds. **38**   Any attempt to borrow more than the setting from a game is probably doomed.

There are many examples of successful film-game combinations. Rather than making a film using characters and stories from a computer game, the trick seems to be to make a film that has a fast-moving action sequence and then bring out a game based on that sequence. People who enjoyed the film will probably want to buy the game. This clearly creates a new market opportunity for the gaming industry.

Why do gamers feel disappointed by films based on their favourite games? **39**   Computer games can show the action from a number of perspectives easily, because everything is computer-generated. But filming a sequence from 20 different cameras would cost a fortune, so it simply isn't done in the film version – leaving the gamers feeling that the film didn't look as real as the computer game.

Cameras matter in another sense, too. In a film the director shows you the action from certain perspectives but makes sure he doesn't show you some things to keep you in suspense. Think of your favourite thriller. **40**   In films you are not supposed to have access to all the information. Suspense and mystery are essential elements of film-making.

41   When you play a game, you have to do certain tasks to proceed to the next level. Therefore, you must be able to see everything in order to make your choices, to decide what to do next: which door to open, and so on. You must have access to all the information. You, as the player, are always in control. In the cinema you never control the action. You just sit and watch.

There can be some interaction between films and computer games on a number of different levels, but in the end they fulfil different needs. **42**   For all the similarities between technologies and special effects, we shouldn't forget that a story and a game are fundamentally different.

A We go to the cinema to let someone else tell us a story, knowing we can't influence what happens at all.

B You wouldn't be interested in watching the film if you knew the identity of the murderer, for instance.

C This is not true for computer games.

D Its success lies in the use of special effects.

E This usually means that the film has a good chance of being as commercially successful as the game on which it is based.

F One reason is technical.

G However, the difficulty for the producers of Hollywood appears to be knowing where and when to stop.

Essential tips

▸ Look at the text to see what it is about. Even without the missing sentences, you can understand the general meaning.

▸ Read the text before and after each gap. Try to guess what the missing information is.

▸ Go through the gapped sentences. Try to find a link between the text and the gapped sentences.

▸ The text and the gapped sentence will be on the same topic.

▸ Re-read the whole text to make sure it makes sense.

Question 37: The sentence before the gap talks about guaranteeing *a large audience*. If a film has a large audience, what is it? Find an option that defines what it is.

Question 40: What kind of film is a thriller? Which sentence option refers to one?

Question 41: The last sentence of the paragraph before the gap talks about 'essential elements of film-making'. The next paragraph talks about computer games. Which sentence option makes a suitable topic sentence for this paragraph?

For the Glossary see page 27 ▶

PAPER 1	Reading and ▶	Part 1
	Use of English	Part 2
PAPER 2	Writing	Part 3
		Part 4
PAPER 3	Listening	Part 5
PAPER 4	Speaking	Part 6
		Part 7

You are going to read a magazine article in which four young people talk about how their parents' careers have influenced them. For questions **43–52**, choose from the people (**A–D**). The people may be chosen more than once.

Mark your answers **on the separate answer sheet**.

Which person

thinks his or her parent's job is boring?	**43**	
was discouraged from following the same profession?	**44**	
changed his or her mind about a future career?	**45**	
experienced pressure to follow the same profession?	**46**	
feels he or she has not been influenced in choosing a career?	**47**	
comes from a long line of people in this profession?	**48**	
thinks the profession in question offers few opportunities?	**49**	
is concerned his or her choice will cause an argument?	**50**	
thinks that success in his or her parent's profession is difficult?	**51**	
thinks his or her parent's profession is rewarding?	**52**	

Essential tips

▸ Skim through the whole text to get a general idea.

▸ Read the questions and underline the key words. Make sure you understand the exact meaning of each question.

▸ Look quickly through the text for information about the key words in each question. Remember that the key words might not be in the text at all, but there will be other words or expressions with that meaning.

▸ If you find a text where the key words are mentioned, look through the other texts as well to make sure you have got the correct answer.

Question 43: This person thinks their parent's job is *boring*. What is the key word and what are synonyms for it?

Question 48: If someone comes from *a long line* of people in a certain profession, who else was in that profession?

Question 52: There are different ways to say that something is *rewarding*. In which text can you find reference to this?

For the Glossary see page 27 ▶

A chip off the old block

How much are children influenced in their choice of profession by their parents' jobs?
We asked four young people about their experience.

A Graham Button

My dad is a self-employed builder, like his father and his grandfather, and that means he was often out working in the evenings or at weekends when I was a child. I think he was proud of doing a 'real' job, something with his hands, which is perhaps why he always tried to push me into taking up the same profession. And of course he had his own business, which he wanted me to continue after he retired. When I was in high school, I decided that I really didn't want to go into the family business, so at the moment I'm studying history. My father probably thinks I'm going to become a partner in his firm after I graduate, so I do worry that we might have a big fight about this some time in the future.

B Sue Smith

My mother's a nuclear physicist, which sounds very exciting. The truth is it's a pretty tough profession. And I just don't think it's a very interesting job. Of course it's important, but as far as I can see, you spend most of the day at a desk doing hundreds of calculations, and then checking and rechecking them. My mother did try to motivate me to take an interest in science subjects when I was about 14 or 15, and I think she'd be secretly pleased if I wanted to be a scientist, but she's never put any sort of pressure on me. But I know she also thinks – as I do – that there aren't so many jobs available in pure research, which is what she does.

C Barry Porter

When people find out my mother's an actress, they always ask what Hollywood films she's been in, and I have to explain that she's only ever worked in provincial theatres. She's hardly ever been on television, which is why not many people know her. That's one of the problems with the theatre: very few people get to the top of the profession, and you have to be extremely lucky just to make a living from it. Actors often worry about where the next job's coming from. Even if I had any talent for acting, I'd be put off by that side of it. As you can gather, I really don't think my future is in the theatre, and in any case my mother has always tried to steer me away from taking up the profession.

D Ruth Lawrence

My father teaches maths at high school, which definitely used to come in handy when we had a maths test the next day! I think in the back of his mind he expected me to be good at maths because he was always there to explain it. The truth is I've always been terrible at the subject. He also used to tell me about the satisfaction you can get from teaching, and I do think he's right about that. I used to think I wanted to be a teacher, but then I began to think of the disadvantages. The profession's changed and these days teachers have to work a lot in the holidays and prepare a lot at home. In the end I decided to go into accounting, and I don't really think my dad's job affected my decision at all.

PAPER 1 Reading and
Use of English

PAPER 2 Writing ▶ Part 1
Part 2

PAPER 3 Listening

PAPER 4 Speaking

You **must** answer this question. Write your answer in **140–190** words in an appropriate style.

1 In your English class you have been talking about the value of learning a foreign language. Now, your English teacher has asked you to write an essay.

Write an essay using **all** the notes and give reasons for your point of view.

Is it worth learning a foreign language?

Notes
Write about:

1. using a foreign language for work
2. using a foreign language for travel
3. .... (your own idea)

Essential tips

Part 1

▸ Decide whether you think it is worth learning a foreign language and state your opinion clearly in the introduction.

▸ In the body of your essay you need to give reasons to support your argument. Use all of the topics in the notes and put each idea in a separate paragraph. Give examples of why you think (or why you don't think) it is important to learn a foreign language for the purposes of work or travel. You could also consider other people's points of view.

▸ Make sure you include **your own idea** on a third, related topic and use it to support your opinion. For example, you could say that learning a foreign language is also useful for communicating with friends of other nationalities.

▸ Summarise your overall opinion in the final paragraph.

▸ Check the length of your essay, your grammar, spelling and punctuation.

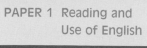
PAPER 1 Reading and
         Use of English
PAPER 2 Writing ▶ Part 1
PAPER 3 Listening   Part 2
PAPER 4 Speaking

Write an answer to **one** of the questions **2–5** in this part. Write your answer in **140–190** words in an appropriate style.

2 You see this notice on your school/college noticeboard:

> **What is your favourite possession?**
>
> Write an article for our student magazine about your favourite possession and say why it is special to you.
>
> We'll publish the most interesting articles in our magazine.

Write your **article**.

3 You have received this email from your English-speaking friend, Maria.

> **From:** Maria
> **Subject:** English course – activities
>
> Hi!
>
> I'm looking forward to the English course we've decided to do! There are classes in the morning and activities in the afternoon. We need to decide whether we do indoor activities, like swimming, or outdoor activities, like horse riding. What do you think we should choose? What kind of activities do you like best?
>
> See you soon!
>
> Maria

Write your **email**.

Essential tips

Part 2

▶ Decide which question you can answer best. Do you have ideas and vocabulary for any of the questions?

▶ Underline the key words in the instructions.

▶ Plan the different sections of your answer and decide on the main point of each paragraph.

▶ Spend some time making notes about each paragraph.

▶ Make sure your ideas are clearly organised. Every paragraph should be on one topic.

▶ Check the length of your answer, your grammar, spelling and punctuation.

Question 2
Use a neutral style. In your introduction you should say briefly what you are going to write about. Make sure you answer the question. Describe your possession in detail. Give some background information to explain what makes it special to you.

Question 3
Use an informal style. Thank Maria for her email and say that you're also looking forward to the English course. In the main body of your email, answer Maria's questions. You could ask Maria some questions, too, for example, does she agree with your choice? In your conclusion, say that you hope to hear from Maria soon. Should you use an informal or formal way to end your email?

Continued on next page ▶

PAPER 1 Reading and
         Use of English

PAPER 2 Writing ▶   Part 1
                         Part 2

PAPER 3 Listening

PAPER 4 Speaking

4 You see this notice in a popular English-language magazine called *Cinema News*:

> Have you seen any good films lately? If you have, write a review for our magazine! Include information on the plot and the characters, and say why you think the film is worth seeing.
>
> We will publish the best reviews in next month's issue.

Write your **review**.

5 (*for FIRST FOR SCHOOLS candidates only*)

Answer the following question based on your reading of **one** of the set books.

If the book you have read were made into a film, which character would be the most interesting? Write a **letter** to an English penfriend who has read the same book, saying which character you imagine would be most interesting in a film and explaining why. Do not write any addresses.

Essential tips

Question 4
You are writing for a popular magazine, so the style of your review could be semi-formal. Organise your ideas in paragraphs and make sure you answer all parts of the question. In the introduction, you could describe the film in general terms (What is the film called? What kind of film is it? Who directed it? Who acts in it?). The main body could consist of two or more paragraphs in which you should describe and comment on the plot and the characters. In the conclusion say why you think the film is worth seeing.

Question 5 (*for FIRST FOR SCHOOLS candidates only*)

The question asks you to think of an interesting character. You don't have to write about the main character. Your letter should be informal.

Essential tips

▸ Look carefully at the question for each listening text and underline the key words.

▸ Read the three options and think of words that are associated with them.

▸ The listening texts are dialogues and monologues. The answer may come at the beginning, in the middle or at the end of the listening text.

▸ Don't worry about understanding every word you hear. Listen for the general meaning.

▸ If you hear a word or phrase from an answer, do not assume that this is the correct answer.

▸ Decide on an option after the first listening. Use the second listening to check your answers.

Question 3: All three options may be discussed in the listening text. You need to decide which of them both speakers say.

Question 6: The question asks what the speaker is doing. You will need to listen to the whole text to understand this, rather than hearing the answer in a single sentence.

Question 7: You need to know how the speaker is feeling. The listening text may not use the same words, so listen carefully for synonyms.

🎧 **Track 1**

You will hear people talking in eight different situations. For questions **1–8**, choose the best answer (**A**, **B** or **C**).

1   You hear a student talking about her college course.
    What does she say about it?
    A   She enjoys seeing how things work in practice.
    B   She is sure she'd like to work in a related field.
    C   She wants to know more about an aspect of the course.

2   You hear a conversation between a customer and a florist.
    What does the customer decide to do?
    A   take the florist's advice
    B   research a new species of rose
    C   buy an expensive bunch of flowers

3   You hear two students discussing their maths class.
    What do they agree about?
    A   how helpful their maths teacher is
    B   how useful the maths phone app is
    C   how difficult the maths topic is

4   You hear a weather forecast on the radio.
    Where are violent storms expected?
    A   the south coast
    B   the east coast
    C   the west coast

5   You hear a woman leaving a message for a plumber.
    The woman wants him to
    A   correct an error he has made.
    B   call her when he finishes work.
    C   discover the source of a problem.

6   You hear a man talking about his travel plans.
    What is he doing?
    A   complaining about train timetables
    B   confirming a hotel reservation
    C   making a request of someone

7   You hear two friends talking about the football team they support.
    How does the man feel?
    A   optimistic about the team's prospects
    B   annoyed by the referee's decision-making
    C   surprised by the goalkeeper's ability

8   You hear part of an interview with a student who wants to become a volunteer.
    What does the student say about it?
    A   He is keen to pass on his knowledge.
    B   He wants to repay the people who helped him.
    C   He regrets not getting involved earlier.

🎧 **Track 2**

You will hear part of a talk by a man called James Edwards, who is the director of a museum association called Museums for All. For questions **9–18**, complete the sentences with a word or short phrase.

Museums for All

The association Museums for All was started

        (9) .... years ago.

James says the task of Museums for All is to change people's

        (10) .... of museum visits.

James worked for a big **(11)** .... company

        before he was offered his current position.

James believes that museums should be more

        (12) .... in the way they attract visitors.

James says that traditional museums used to be aimed at people with a good

        standard of **(13)** ....

To raise interest in museums, James would like museums to have good

        (14) .... with local schools.

James wants museums to be friendly, in the same way that

        (15) .... are.

James says that a trip to the museum can be **(16)** ....

        for some people.

James feels that it is the role of the **(17)** .... to invest

        in rebuilding museums.

The Museum Festival next year will be held in

        (18) ....

Essential tips

▸ Read the instructions and think about the topic before you listen.

▸ Go through the questions carefully and think about the sort of information that is missing.

▸ Remember that the questions follow the order of the text.

▸ You will hear the word or words you need for each question, but the rest of the sentence will be slightly different.

Question 9: What kind of information is missing? The reason why Museums for All was started, the time that it was started or the people who started it?

Question 12: Are you listening for a noun or adjective for this gap?

Question 18: Look at the context. The missing information must be a place or a time.

PAPER 1   Reading and
           Use of English

PAPER 2   Writing

PAPER 3   Listening   ▶

PAPER 4   Speaking

Part 1
Part 2
Part 3
Part 4

🎧 **Track 3**

You will hear five short extracts in which people are talking about school trips they went on when they were younger. For questions **19–23**, choose from the list (**A–H**) what each speaker says. Use the letters only once. There are three extra letters which you do not need to use.

A   I made some new friends.

B   I had some communication problems.

Speaker 1   [   ] 19

C   I would like to go back to the area soon.

Speaker 2   [   ] 20

D   I went on similar trips over the next few years.

Speaker 3   [   ] 21

E   I wasn't properly prepared for the trip.

Speaker 4   [   ] 22

F   I thought the trip was good value for money.

Speaker 5   [   ] 23

G   I thought the trip was too long.

H   I would have liked more independence.

Essential tips

▸   Read the instructions carefully to identify what the speakers will be talking about.

▸   Before you listen, look at each option and think of how these ideas can be expressed.

▸   If a speaker mentions a word from the options, think carefully before you choose that option; it may be that the word is used in a different meaning.

▸   All the speakers will be talking about the same topic. You need to focus on the differences between the speakers.

Option D: If one of the speakers says that he or she *wanted* to go on more trips, or *intended* to do this, does it mean that he or she really did go on more trips?

Option E: The key word here is *prepared*. You can get prepared for a journey in a number of ways: you can start by making plans, getting information or doing some shopping. What else could it mean?

Option H: The key word here is *independence*. What are the synonyms of this word? How else could this be phrased?

PAPER 1 Reading and
Use of English

PAPER 2 Writing

PAPER 3 Listening ▶

PAPER 4 Speaking

Part 1
Part 2
Part 3
Part 4

🎧 **Track 4**

You will hear a radio interview with Julia Emerson, a young writer. For questions **24–30**, choose the best answer (**A, B** or **C**).

24 According to Julia, nowadays Hollywood producers
   A   usually think of ideas for films themselves.
   B   write screenplays and contact stars.
   C   contact agents to find writers for them.

25 Julia says that she
   A   has written a number of successful screenplays for studios.
   B   was lucky enough to have her first screenplay accepted.
   C   was not discouraged by the lack of response from studios.

26 Julia began writing in her spare time when she
   A   published some articles in a magazine.
   B   had an idea for a TV series.
   C   came first in a short-story competition.

27 Julia says that
   A   she would like to write a version of a classic film.
   B   there is a danger she might imitate other films.
   C   creative people should think a lot about films.

28 Julia's screenplay is about two sisters who
   A   set out to try living in the jungle.
   B   find themselves in a difficult situation.
   C   end up hating each other.

29 The theme of the story is
   A   how our emotions about our family can change.
   B   Julia's relationship with her brothers and sisters.
   C   about the importance of having a family.

30 It appears that the film based on Julia's screenplay
   A   must be made within the next few months.
   B   will be made when the studio has paid Julia.
   C   might never be made.

Essential tips

▶ Read the questions or question stems carefully.

▶ Read the options carefully and underline the key words.

▶ Be careful: an option may include words or phrases from the recording, but this does not necessarily mean that the option is correct.

▶ The questions follow the order of the text.

Question 24: Who do you expect writes the screenplay for a film? Is this the same person who thinks of the idea for a film? The correct answer may be different from what you think, so listen carefully.

Question 26: Aspects of all the options are heard in the listening text, but only one option completes the stem correctly.

Question 28: The correct answer summarises the story of the film. Which option does that?

Part 1 (2 minutes)

The examiner (interlocutor) will ask each of you to speak briefly in turn and to give personal information about yourselves. You can expect a variety of questions, such as:

Can you describe the area where you live?
What do you like and dislike about this area? (Why?)
How do you think the area could be improved?
Where else would you like to live? (Why?)

Part 2 (4 minutes)

You will each be asked to talk for a minute without interruption. You will each be given two different photographs in turn to talk about. After your partner has finished speaking, you will be asked a brief question connected with your partner's photographs.

1 Places to live

Look at the two photographs on page 159 which show different types of accommodation.

Candidate A, compare the photographs, and say why you think people have chosen to live in these places.

Candidate B, which of these would you prefer to live in? (Why?)

2 Audiences

Look at the two photographs on page 160 which show people at concerts.

Candidate B, compare the photographs, and say how you think the people are feeling.

Candidate A, which of these events would you prefer to go to? (Why?)

Essential tips

Part 1

▶ Try to sound natural. Don't learn a speech off by heart.

▶ Avoid one- or two-word answers or answers that are long and complicated.

▶ You can prepare for this part of the interview by making sure you can talk about yourself, your home, your family, your hobbies, etc.

▶ Listen carefully to the question and answer exactly what is asked.

Part 2

▶ In this part you must compare the two colour photographs you are given. When you compare them say what the two photographs have in common and how they are different.

▶ Listen carefully to what the examiner asks you to do. After comparing the photographs the examiner will ask you to comment and give your personal reaction to them.

▶ You are supposed to speak for a full minute. Practise speaking for a minute, so you know how this feels.

▶ The examiner will ask you to comment on your partner's photographs. You have about 30 seconds for this.

▶ Don't interrupt when your partner is speaking. Use a few sentences to answer the question you are asked after your partner has spoken.

Part 3 (4 minutes)

You will be asked to discuss something together without interruption by the examiner. You will have a page of ideas and a question to help you.

A camping trip

Imagine you're going on a camping trip to the mountains. Turn to page 161 which shows ideas for items you could take with you and a question for you to discuss. Talk to each other about how each item could be useful during the trip. Then decide which **two** of these items you would take on your camping trip.

Part 4 (4 minutes)

The examiner will encourage you to develop the topic of your discussion in Part 3 by asking questions, such as:

Would you enjoy a camping holiday? (Why? / Why not?)
What other type of holiday would you enjoy? (Why?)
Would you prefer to go on holiday with your family or with a group of friends?
(Why? / Why not?)
What is the best time of year to go on a holiday? (Why?)
Is it usual for people in your country to visit other countries on holiday?
What's a typical kind of holiday for someone in your country?

Essential tips

Part 3

▶ Work together with your partner. Discuss the question and the ideas and decide on an answer together.

▶ Involve your partner in the discussion. Your contribution and your partner's contribution to the discussion should be equal.

▶ Practise expressions used for giving your opinion and agreeing/disagreeing, such as *in my opinion*, *I'm afraid I don't agree*, etc.

▶ Don't make a decision too quickly. Look at the ideas first, give your opinion about them, ask your partner's opinion and then make a decision.

▶ Remember you don't have to agree with your partner. What is more important is reaching a decision.

Part 4

▶ Don't interrupt when your partner is speaking, but be ready to give your opinion after your partner has finished.

▶ It doesn't matter if you agree or disagree with your partner, but it is important to give reasons for your opinion.

PAPER 1 Reading and Use of English

▶▶ PART 5

adore (v) to like very much, to love deeply

supreme (adj) the greatest, the best

hulk (n) something or someone large and awkward

take a hit (phr) to be hit by someone

smack (v) to hit with force

immense (adj) extremely large

subtlety (n) the quality of not being noticeable or obvious in any way

gain (v) to achieve

readership (n) the people who read a certain newspaper, people who regularly buy a magazine

stock (n) one's parents, grandparents and other older or past relatives, sometimes including an entire race

bully (v) to force others to do things

turning point (n) the point at which a very significant change occurs, a decisive moment

the ropes (phr) all the things one needs to know in order to do a job or deal with something

dissuade (v) to persuade someone not to do something

insistent (adj) demanding over and over again that something should happen

quit (v) to give up an activity

resent (v) to feel anger at something, to feel hurt about something

abandon (v) to leave someone or something when you should stay with them and look after them

▶▶ PART 6

turnover (n) the amount of annual business

grandly (adv) suggesting that something or someone has great importance

interactive (adj) describes a system or computer program designed to involve the user in the exchange of information

harvest (v) to collect or receive the benefits of something

stunning (adj) very beautiful, very surprising

sequence (n) a part of a film that shows a particular event or a related series of events

gravity (n) a natural force pulling objects to the ground

discard (v) to throw away, to dispose of

leap (v) to jump, to bound

rippling (adj) moving in small waves

segment (n) a separate piece, a section of something

comprise (v) to include, to contain

set (v) if a film is set in a place or period of time, it happens there or at that time

doom (v) to send to an unhappy, inescapable end (failure, ruin, destruction, etc.)

perspective (n) a way of seeing things, a point of view

fulfil (v) to satisfy, to accomplish

fundamentally (adv) basically, essentially

▶▶ PART 7

chip off the old block (phr) a child whose appearance or character closely resembles that of one or the other parent

self-employed (adj) working for yourself and not employed by a single company

take up (phr v) to enter into a profession or business

retire (v) to leave the work force and stop working

tough (adj) difficult, demanding

motivate (v) to encourage, to stimulate

research (n) a study of something

provincial (adj) relating to an area which is governed as part of a country or an empire

put off (phr v) to annoy or disgust

steer (v) to guide someone by gently pushing or leading

come in handy (phr) to be useful

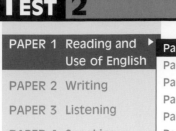

PAPER 1	Reading and	▶	Part 1
	Use of English		Part 2
PAPER 2	Writing		Part 3
			Part 4
PAPER 3	Listening		Part 5
PAPER 4	Speaking		Part 6
			Part 7

For questions **1–8**, read the text below and decide which answer (**A**, **B**, **C** or **D**) best fits each gap. There is an example at the beginning (**0**).

Mark your answers **on the separate answer sheet**.

Example:

0 **A** quantity   **B** piece   **C** unit   **D** part

Essential tips

Question 2: Which of the four verbs collocates with *weight*?

Question 5: Look at the context. Is it a good thing that diets don't work for most people? Does the missing word have a positive or negative meaning?

Question 6: Which of the four nouns can be followed by the preposition *to* and a gerund?

Going on a diet

A calorie is a (**0**)........ for measuring the amount of energy food will produce. The average person needs about 1,800 calories per day to stay healthy. Without energy, the heart cannot (**1**) .... blood through blood vessels and the organs cannot function.

You (**2**)........ weight because you consume more calories a day than your body requires. The only way to lose weight is to (**3**)........ the number of calories you consume. This is the basic (**4**) .... behind most diets.

(**5**) .... , diets don't work for most people. It's not that they don't lose weight: they do, but when they go off the diet, the kilos creep back. The (**6**) .... to losing weight and maintaining weight loss is a sensible diet and exercise plan. You need to work out how to eat fewer calories than you (**7**) .... consume. You should also exercise daily so you can use up calories. Burning 250 or 500 calories per day can (**8**) .... a big difference.

1	**A** pump	**B** pull	**C** drag	**D** force
2	**A** make	**B** increase	**C** gain	**D** put
3	**A** shrink	**B** take	**C** remove	**D** reduce
4	**A** way	**B** principle	**C** method	**D** kind
5	**A** Similarly	**B** Though	**C** Unfortunately	**D** Although
6	**A** key	**B** secret	**C** way	**D** idea
7	**A** preferably	**B** actually	**C** consistently	**D** eventually
8	**A** have	**B** do	**C** make	**D** give

PAPER 1	Reading and Use of English ▶	Part 1
		Part 2
PAPER 2	Writing	Part 3
		Part 4
PAPER 3	Listening	Part 5
PAPER 4	Speaking	Part 6
		Part 7

For questions **9–16**, read the text below and think of the word which best fits each gap. Use only **one** word in each gap. There is an example at the beginning (**0**).

Write your answers **IN CAPITAL LETTERS on the separate answer sheet**.

Example: | 0 | M | A | N | Y | | | | | | | | | | | | | | | | | | |

I'm not superstitious, honestly!

How (**0**) .... people could truly say they are not superstitious? A recent survey shows that almost 90% of people believe in one sort of superstition (**9**) .... another and say that it influences their lives.

One of the questions people (**10**) .... asked is whether they saw themselves as lucky or unlucky. Their answers turned out to be the most interesting aspect of this survey. Nearly two-thirds (**11**) .... those taking part said they believed that people were naturally lucky or unlucky.

Professor Morgan Howard, (**12**) .... analysed the results of the survey, was fascinated by this finding, so he went a step further and asked these people (**13**) .... kind of superstitions they believed in. (**14**) .... his surprise, he discovered that almost all the people who regarded themselves (**15**) .... lucky believed in positive superstitions. They did things to promote their good luck, such as crossing their fingers. (**16**) .... would appear that people make their own luck by their attitude to life.

Essential tips

Question 10: Is the verb *ask* being used in the active or the passive form here?

Question 13: The gap is part of an indirect question about the kind of superstitions people believe in.

Question 15: The gap follows a verb, *regard*, and a reflexive pronoun, *themselves*. What preposition comes after *regard* + object?

PAPER 1   Reading and ▸ | Part 1
          Use of English | Part 2
PAPER 2   Writing | Part 3
          | Part 4
PAPER 3   Listening | Part 5
          | Part 6
PAPER 4   Speaking | Part 7

For questions **17–24**, read the text below. Use the word given in capitals at the end of some of the lines to form a word that fits in the gap **in the same line**. There is an example at the beginning (**0**).

Write your answers **IN CAPITAL LETTERS on the separate answer sheet.**

Example: | 0 | R | E | C | E | N | T | L | Y | | | | | | | | |

Essential tips

Question 17: The missing word is a verb. What verb form do you need?

Question 19: The gap is between the auxiliary (*have*) and the main verb (*discovered*), so it must be an adverb.

Question 24: Read the sentence carefully. It says *a large number of*. Do you need the singular or plural form of a noun?

Wild animals

Wild animals have (**0**) …….. made an appearance in the back   **RECENT**

gardens of American suburbs. They have caused havoc and

have (**17**) …….. domestic pets.   **THREAT**

Mountain lions that wander into suburbs are now quite

(**18**) …….. to attack humans, which is worrying, while bears   **WILL**

and wolves have (**19**) …….. discovered rubbish bins. If you   **APPARENT**

find the (**20**) …….. of your bin scattered all over the garden   **CONTAIN**

one morning, there is a distinct (**21**) …….. that a bear   **POSSIBLE**

has been feasting there during the night.

Nobody should be particularly surprised by this development,

which was predicted by experts years ago, and it's not

(**22**) …….. under the circumstances. One cause is the massive   **EXPECT**

expansion of (**23**) …….. into areas that were wild and   **HOUSE**

uninhabited not long ago. In addition, over the past few decades

a large number of (**24**) …….. have been placed on hunting   **RESTRICT**

certain animals, allowing their populations to grow. It looks as

if humans will simply have to get used to their new neighbours.

PAPER 1	Reading and ▶	Part 1
	Use of English	Part 2
PAPER 2	Writing	Part 3
		Part 4
PAPER 3	Listening	Part 5
		Part 6
PAPER 4	Speaking	Part 7

For questions **25–30**, complete the second sentence so that it has a similar meaning to the first sentence, using the word given. **Do not change the word given.** You must use between **two** and **five** words, including the word given. Here is an example (**0**).

Example:

0   I'll be very happy when I go on holiday.

FORWARD

I'm .... on holiday.

The gap can be filled by the words 'looking forward to going' so you write:

Example: | 0 | LOOKING FORWARD TO GOING

Write **only** the missing words **IN CAPITAL LETTERS on the separate answer sheet.**

Essential tips

Question 25: What is the opposite of *cheap*? How can 'as' be used with an adjective?

Question 26: If someone didn't do something and you think this was wrong, what modal verb can you use?

Question 29: What structure do we use after *asked* to report a request? How do we report a negative request?

25   The phone was cheaper than I expected.

AS

The phone was .... I expected.

26   Why didn't you tell me I was wrong?

TOLD

You .... I was wrong.

27   She found the photographs when she was cleaning her room.

CAME

She .... when she was cleaning her room.

28   How many portraits did Picasso paint?

BY

How many portraits .... Picasso?

29   'Please don't stay out late,' his mother said.

ASKED

His mother .... out late.

30   I'd rather not go out this afternoon.

FEEL

I .... out this afternoon.

PAPER 1 Reading and
    Use of English

PAPER 2 Writing

PAPER 3 Listening

PAPER 4 Speaking

Part 1
Part 2
Part 3
Part 4
Part 5
Part 6
Part 7

You are going to read an article about life in the countryside. For questions **31–36**, choose the answer (**A**, **B**, **C** or **D**) which you think fits best according to the text.

Mark your answers **on the separate answer sheet**.

How I came to envy the country mice

I have been living in London for more than 60 years, but still, when I'm driving and take some clever back-street short cut, I catch myself thinking: how extraordinary that it is me doing this! For a moment the town mouse I have become is being seen by the country mouse I used to be. And although, given a new start, I would again become a town mouse, when I visit relations in the country, I envy them.

Recently, I stood beside a freshwater lake in Norfolk, made by diverting a small river, near where my brother lives. As he was identifying some of the birds we could see, in came seven swans. They circled, then the haunting sound of their wing beats gave way to silence as they glided down for splashdown.

It is not a 'picturesque' part of the coast, but it has a definite character of line and light and colour. 'You do live in a lovely place,' I said to my brother, and he answered, 'Yes, I do.' There are probably few days when he does not pause to recognise its loveliness as he works with his boats – he teaches sailing – or goes about his many other occupations.

The lake's creator is a local landowner, continuing a tradition whereby the nature of our countryside has been determined by those who own the land. Formerly, landowners would almost certainly have made such changes for their own benefit, but this time it was done to help preserve the wildlife here, which is available for any visitor to see, providing they do nothing to disturb the birds. It is evidence of change: country life is changing fast.

line 15

One of the biggest changes I have witnessed is that second-homers, together with commuters, have come to be accepted as a vital part of the country scene. And the men and women who service their cars, dig their gardens, lay their carpets and do all the other things they need are vital to modern country life. It is quite likely that the children of today's workers may be moving into the same kind of jobs as the second-homers and the retired. Both the children of a country woman I know are at university, and she herself, now that they have left home, is working towards a university degree.

Much depends, of course, on the part of the countryside you are living in and on personality – your own and that of your neighbours. In my brother's Norfolk village, social life seems dizzying to a Londoner. In addition to dropping in on neighbours, people throw and attend parties far more often than we do. My brother's wife Mary and her friends are always going into Norwich for a concert or to King's Lynn for an exhibition. The boring country life that people from cities talk about is a thing of the past – or perhaps it was always mainly in their minds.

This is very unlike living in a London street for 50 years and only knowing the names of four other residents. In these 50 years I have made only one real friend among them. I do enjoy my life, and Mary says that she sometimes envies it (the grass on the other side of the fence ...); but whenever I go to Norfolk, I end up feeling that the lives of country mice are more admirable than my own.

Essential tips

▸ After reading the text for general understanding, read each question and see if you can locate the answer in the text. When you locate the answer in the text, underline it. Some questions refer to specific lines in the text (Question 33), while others refer to specific paragraphs (Question 36).

▸ Look carefully at the key words in the four options. For example, in question 31, option A, the key words are *driving through back streets* and *source of surprise*. This option can only be correct if the writer does drive through back streets and is surprised to find herself doing this.

Question 32: The text refers to the *sound* of the swans landing. Does it say that the sound was very loud, in which case *deafening* would be the correct answer? How is 'haunting' used here?

Question 34: The question asks you what is *suggested* about outsiders. This means the answer is not clearly stated in the text. You need to 'read between the lines' and see what is implied in the text.

Question 36: The answer to this question can be found in the whole of the last paragraph.

31 It is sometimes a source of surprise to the writer

A to find herself driving through back streets.
B that she has been in the city for so long.
C to realise how much she has got used to living in London.
D that she lives in the city when she prefers the country.

32 The atmosphere created by the writer when she describes the swans is

A moving.
B frightening.
C deafening.
D disturbing.

33 What does 'It' in line 15 refer to?

A the lake
B the fact that the lake belongs to a landowner here
C the reason for the landowner's action
D the fact that wildlife now needs to be preserved

34 What is suggested about outsiders who now live in the country?

A that country people no longer reject them
B that they often do work like servicing cars and digging gardens
C that the men and women who work for them are from the city
D that many of them have been in the countryside for a long time

35 Social life in the country

A depends completely on where you live.
B is not as boring as people in cities think it is.
C is not affected by your neighbours.
D is always less exciting than life in the city.

36 What do we learn about the writer's attitude to London in the final paragraph?

A She can't adjust to living in London.
B She has regretted moving to London.
C The people in her street are unusually unfriendly.
D Life there is very different to country life.

For the Glossary see page 47 ▶

PAPER 1 Reading and ▸   Part 1
Use of English   Part 2

PAPER 2 Writing   Part 3

Part 4

PAPER 3 Listening   Part 5

Part 6

PAPER 4 Speaking

Part 7

You are going to read an article about the evolution of hands. Six sentences have been removed from the article. Choose from the sentences **A–G** the one which fits each gap (**37–42**). There is one extra sentence which you do not need to use.

Mark your answers **on the separate answer sheet**.

Our amazing hands

The hand is where the mind meets the world. We use our hands to build fires, to steer airplanes, to write. The human brain, with its open-ended creativity, may be the thing that makes our species unique. But without hands, all the grand ideas we think up would come to nothing.

The reason we can use our hands for so many things is their extraordinary anatomy. **37** Some are connected to bones within the hand, while others snake their way to the arm. The wrist is a floating group of bones and ligaments threaded with blood vessels and nerves. The nerves send branches into each fingertip. The hand can generate fine forces or huge ones. A watchmaker can use his hands to set springs in place under a microscope. A sportsman can use the same anatomy to throw a ball at over 100 kilometres an hour.

Other species have hands too. **38** In other cases we have to look closer. A bat's wings may look like sheets of skin. But underneath, a bat has the same five fingers as a human, as well as a wrist connected to the same cluster of wrist bones connected to the same long bones of the arm.

In exploring how hands have evolved, researchers over the past 150 years have dug up fossils on every continent. They've compared the anatomy of hands in living animals. They've studied the genes that build hands. It appears that our hands began to evolve at least 380 million years ago from fins – not the flat, ridged fins of a goldfish but the muscular, stout fins of extinct relatives of today's lungfish. Inside these were a few chunky bones corresponding to the bones in our arms. **39** The digits later emerged and became separate, allowing the animals to grip underwater vegetation as they clambered through it.

40 Some species had seven fingers. Others had eight. But by the time vertebrates were walking around on dry land 340 million years ago, the hand had been scaled back to only five fingers. It has retained that number of fingers ever since – for reasons scientists don't yet know.

Nevertheless, there are still many different types of hands in living species, from dolphin flippers to eagle wings to the hanging hooks of sloths. **41** They can also see that despite the outward differences, all hands start out in much the same way. There is a network of many genes that builds a hand, and all hands are built by variations on that same network. It takes only subtle changes in these genes to make fingers longer or to turn nails into claws.

The discovery of the molecular toolbox for hand building has given scientists a deeper understanding of evolution. **42** It may just be a little more of one protein here, a little less of another there. In the past, scientists could recognise only the outward signs that hands had evolved from a common ancestor. Today scientists are uncovering the inward signs as well.

A Over time, smaller ones developed that would eventually become wrists and fingers.

B Although a vulture's wing and a lion's paw may appear to have nothing in common, the difference between them may come down to tiny variations.

C They also use them for a number of different purposes.

D No one would doubt that the five fingers at the end of an orangutan's arm are part of anything else.

E By studying these, scientists are beginning to understand the molecular changes that led to such dramatic variations.

F The thumb alone is controlled by nine separate muscles.

G Early hands were more exotic than any hand today.

Essential tips

▶ Read the main text from which paragraphs have been gapped to get the general idea.

▶ Look carefully at the sentences before and after the gap. Are there any words that show you what the missing sentence is about?

▶ There are many ways you can link parts of a text. It could be a contrast, a comparison, an example, etc. Look for linking expressions that connect ideas in a text.

▶ Pay special attention to nouns, pronouns, words like *this* and *that* and any other words or phrases that refer to what has gone before or what comes after them.

Question 37: The sentence before the gap says the hand is amazingly constructed (*their extraordinary anatomy*). The sentence option that fits this gap is an example of this and links with the sentence after the gap.

Question 38: The sentence before the gap mentions other species. Two sentence options refer to other species, but only one links with the sentence after the gap.

Question 41: The sentence before the gap describes different types of *hands*. The sentence option that fits this gap refers to these different types of hands. In the sentence after the gap, who does 'they' refer to?

For the Glossary see page 47 ▶

You are going to read an article about the activities organised by four schools for Environmental Awareness Day. For questions **43–52** choose from the schools (**A–D**). The schools may be chosen more than once.

Mark your answers **on the separate answer sheet**.

Which school

became better known after Environmental Awareness Day?	**43**
provided online information about the environment?	**44**
asked a specialist to give a talk?	**45**
raised money to help an organisation?	**46**
organised a trip to study animals by the sea?	**47**
is following changes in general weather conditions?	**48**
carried out a project about endangered animals and plants?	**49**
arranged a talk on pollution and local architecture?	**50**
decided to protect a local historical site?	**51**
is located in the centre of the city?	**52**

Essential tips

▸ Read the questions first, and underline key words. Make sure you understand what the question asks.

▸ Locate the answers in the text and underline them.

▸ When you read the text, look for words/phrases which express similar ideas. Do not look for identical words.

Question 44: How can we provide online information?

Question 46: How can a school raise money? When you try to locate the answer, do not look for the verb *raise*. Look for the idea of *raising money*.

Question 48: Can you find another way of saying *general weather conditions*?

For the Glossary see page 47 ▶

Environmental Awareness Day

A Plumpton High School

This school decided to arrange a variety of activities, some aimed at achieving a better understanding of environmental problems, and others designed to be of practical help. For instance, the school magazine brought out a special edition on the subject, full of articles and stories where pupils expressed their feelings about the threats facing our environment. In another attempt to find out for themselves how serious these threats really are, the pupils decided to study the problem of pollution by making a survey, run by the science department, into air pollution in the local shopping centre. The school also held a sponsored walk and handed over nearly £1000 to the World Wide Fund for Nature. Pupils prepared a campaign to ban cars from the city centre and reduce traffic congestion. They gained a lot of publicity for the school by cycling through the city and handing out brochures about the benefits of cycling and walking.

B Cresswell College

The staff and students at Cresswell College held a meeting and discussed a number of suggestions. The most popular suggestion turned out to be the most practical one; it was decided that the local environment should be brightened up. Teams were sent out to plant flowers and young trees on areas of land in the neighbourhood. Senior students monitored the progress of species threatened with extinction and prepared a report on their findings. It was hoped that this would help publicise the problem. A leading expert on wild birds was invited to come and give a talk about the dangers faced by these creatures. He explained the importance of the food chain and asked people to support local wildlife reserves.

C Grayner Institute

This school had already been involved in some projects connected with the environment, though naturally efforts were increased for Environmental Awareness Day. For the last two years the school had been studying the effects of variations in climatic patterns around the world and how these can affect wildlife. A film about those magnificent marine mammals, whales, which was shown to the whole school as part of Environmental Awareness Day, was received with great enthusiasm by pupils. Meredith Summers was invited to talk about how pollution can destroy buildings in the region. Following that, pupils decided to launch a campaign for the restoration of the medieval square in the city centre and asked local authorities to support them financially.

D Halliwell Academy

The pupils at this inner-city secondary school felt that the best way to mark Environmental Awareness Day would be to help people in the area understand how important the environment is to them. One suggestion that was greeted with enthusiasm was to measure the levels of noise in Stanley Road, a busy local shopping street. The information was then placed on a website that the school had started. In order to give them a chance to see for themselves the problems facing some local species, the school took pupils to the coastal marshes of Easton. Many pupils reported afterwards that they had never realised how terrible the effects of pollution could be on coastal wildlife.

PAPER 1   Reading and
          Use of English

PAPER 2   Writing   ▶   Part 1
                             Part 2

PAPER 3   Listening

PAPER 4   Speaking

You **must** answer this question. Write your answer in **140–190** words in an appropriate style.

1   In your English class you have been talking about where people shop. Now, your English teacher has asked you to write an essay.

    Write an essay using **all** the notes and give reasons for your point of view.

> Is it better to shop in small local shops or big supermarkets?
>
> **Notes**
> Write about:
>
> 1. goods available
> 2. prices
> 3. .... (your own idea)

Essential tips

▶   Decide if you prefer small local shops or big supermarkets and state your opinion clearly in the introduction.

▶   In the body of your essay you need to give reasons for your choice. Remember to use all the topics in the notes. If you prefer local shops even though they do not have the range of goods available in a supermarket, you could say why it isn't necessary for them to have several varieties of each type of item. You could also give examples of things that local shops sell that can't be found in supermarkets.

▶   Make sure you include **another topic** (your own idea) and use it to support your opinion. For example, you could say that local shops are **more convenient** because they are close to people's homes (or if you prefer supermarkets, you could say it's **more convenient** to get everything you need in one place). You could talk about how friendly and helpful **staff** tend to be in the two different types of shops.

▶   Summarise your overall opinion in the final paragraph.

PAPER 1 Reading and Use of English

PAPER 2 Writing ▶ Part 1
                     Part 2

PAPER 3 Listening

PAPER 4 Speaking

Essential tips

Question 2

Think of famous people from your country. It could be a historical figure or someone alive today. Do you know enough relevant vocabulary about one of them to write a good letter?

Think about why this person is famous. Give as many reasons as you can.

Is this person popular or unpopular? Say why people have this opinion of the person.

Question 4 (*for FIRST candidates only*)

Think of different sorts of things that families can do in their spare time: hobbies, sports, going out with friends, etc.

Try to organise this information in a clear way for the reader. How many paragraphs will you need? Think of appropriate headings for each of the paragraphs.

Summarise your findings in the final paragraph and make recommendations for improvements to local facilities.

Write an answer to **one** of the questions **2–5** in this part. Write your answer in **140–190** words in an appropriate style.

2   This is part of a letter you receive from Fran, your Australian friend.

> I'm doing a college project on famous people in different countries. Could you tell me about someone famous in your country. Why is this person famous? What do people in your country think about this person?
>
> Thanks!
>
> Fran

Write your **letter**.

3   You see this notice on an English-language website:

> **Reviews wanted   Comedy TV Series**
>
> Write us a review of a TV series that makes people laugh. Your review should include information about the storyline and the characters. Why do people think this TV series is funny? What do you think about the series?

Write your **review**.

4   (*for FIRST candidates only*)

Your college English-language magazine has asked you to write a report on the spare-time activities that are typical of families in your area. Include information on what people do, where they go, and whether local facilities used by families could be improved.

Write your **report**.

Continued on next page ▶

PAPER 1   Reading and
          Use of English

PAPER 2   Writing ▶   Part 1
                        Part 2
PAPER 3   Listening

PAPER 4   Speaking

Essential tips

Question 4 (*for FIRST FOR SCHOOLS candidates only*)

Think of a way to link the content of your story with the title. What kind of noise did Tim hear? What happened when he went outside? Decide on the characters and the setting.

Is your story going to be told in the first person (*I*) or third person (*he*)?

The events in your story should appear in a logical sequence. Use narrative tenses and time expressions to tell your story effectively.

Question 5 (*for FIRST FOR SCHOOLS candidates only*)

If the book is performed as a play, it will have to be much shorter. Could it work with just a few main scenes?

A play can't have too many characters. Think of the characters in the book. Are they intriguing characters? How many of them are there in the book?

A play has to be short and exciting. Are there interesting scenes in the book that could be effective on stage?

4   (*for FIRST FOR SCHOOLS candidates only*)

You see this announcement in an English-language magazine for teenagers.

Stories wanted

Write a story for our short-story competition! Your story must begin with this sentence:

As soon as he heard the noise, Tim ran outside to see what was happening.

Your story must include:
*   TV cameras
*   a surprise

Write your **story**.

5   (*for FIRST FOR SCHOOLS candidates only*)

Answer the following question based on your reading of **one** of the set books.

Your English class is thinking of performing the book or short story you have read as a play. Your English teacher has emailed everyone in your class asking whether you think this is a good idea. Write an **email** to your teacher giving the reasons for your opinion.

Part 1
Part 2
Part 3
Part 4

Track 5

You will hear people talking in eight different situations. For questions **1–8,** choose the best answer (**A**, **B** or **C**).

Essential tips

▶ If you are listening for numbers or dates, you may not hear the number or date you want, but you will hear some information that will tell you the answer. For example, you may hear: 'My birthday is not in March. It's a month later.' In this case the birthday is in April, but you don't actually hear the word 'April'.

▶ Look carefully at questions that have two parts. In Question 7, for example, you must listen for a road which is blocked, and it must be blocked by a crash. If a road is blocked, but not by a crash, this is not the correct answer.

Question 3: Be careful. The speaker does not say the date, but gives information about it (*two years later*).

Question 5: All three options are mentioned. Which of the three is the correct answer?

Question 7: What other words could you hear instead of *crash* that have the same meaning?

1 You hear a physiotherapist talking to a patient.
   What kind of exercises does she recommend?
   A exercises done while lying on the back
   B exercises done while standing up
   C exercises done while lying on the stomach

2 You hear a woman phoning an Indian restaurant to order a takeaway meal.
   Which curry has rice included?
   A beef
   B lamb
   C chicken

3 You hear a woman in an art gallery talking about a painting.
   What date was it painted?
   A 1848
   B 1884
   C 1888

4 You hear a man giving directions to a football ground.
   What does he say the other person must do at the traffic lights?
   A turn left
   B go straight on
   C turn right

5 You hear two colleagues talking about a character one has invented.
   What animal is this character supposed to be?
   A an elephant
   B a horse
   C a bear

6 You hear a woman talking to a policeman at a police station.
   What is her problem?
   A Her bag has been stolen.
   B Her purse has been stolen.
   C Her camera has been stolen.

7 You hear a radio announcement about traffic.
   Which road has been blocked by a car crash?
   A M63
   B A36
   C B636

8 You hear a woman talking about a slimming diet.
   What does she say about the diet?
   A It can have useful results.
   B It can be extremely harmful.
   C It is scientifically approved.

PAPER 1 Reading and
         Use of English

PAPER 2 Writing

PAPER 3 Listening   ▶
                              Part 1
                              Part 2
PAPER 4 Speaking
                              Part 3
                              Part 4

Essential tips

Questions 10 and 11: The missing information is a number for both questions. Which words in question 11 tell you this?

Question 15: The missing word comes after *more* and is followed by an adjective, so it is likely to be an adjective as well.

🎧 **Track 6**

You will hear a woman called Jane Robertson giving a talk about a language called Gaelic. For questions **9–18**, complete the sentences with a word or short phrase.

Gaelic

Jane is the (**9**) .... of a Gaelic school in Scotland.

Today approximately (**10**) .... people speak Gaelic

in Scotland.

If fewer than (**11**) .... people speak a language,

it is considered dead.

Jane would like to see one-third of people under 25 speaking and

(**12**) .... Gaelic.

If very young children are exposed to a language

(**13**) ...., they can learn it most effectively.

Some parents send their children to Jane's school for

(**14**) .... reasons.

Jane says that two character traits of bilingual children are being more

(**15**) .... and tolerant.

Jane feels very (**16**) .... about the future of Gaelic.

Jane says that what is needed is help from (**17**) ....

With a lot of effort, nowadays 80% of children learn Welsh as a

(**18**) .... language.

🎧 **Track 7**

You will hear five short extracts in which young people who are outstanding at sports are talking about their lives. For questions **19–23**, choose from the list (**A–H**) the comment each speaker makes about his or her attitude to sport. Use the letters only once. There are three extra letters which you do not need to use.

Essential tips

Option A: A *family tradition* must mean that the speaker's parents or family members have been connected with the sport. The adjective *strong* means that at least two family members were involved in the same sport.

Option B: This option mentions *social life*, which means that the speaker practises it regularly with friends or people he/she knows.

Option H: What adjective would be used to describe a competition or athletic event where people from different countries compete together?

A	This sport is a strong family tradition for me.
B	I think of it as part of my social life.
C	I started off wanting to impress my parents.
D	It's an investment for my future.
E	I hope to win a lot of prize money.
F	I like the thrill of knowing I'm the best.
G	I'm grateful for a friend's encouragement.
H	Representing my country is my greatest ambition.

Speaker 1   [19]

Speaker 2   [20]

Speaker 3   [21]

Speaker 4   [22]

Speaker 5   [23]

PAPER 1 Reading and
              Use of English

PAPER 2 Writing

PAPER 3 Listening ▶

PAPER 4 Speaking

Part 1
Part 2
Part 3
Part 4

🎧 **Track 8**

You will hear a radio interview with a man called Sam Hall, who is a mountain climber. For questions **24–30**, choose the best answer (**A**, **B** or **C**).

24 Sam describes mountain climbing as
    A dangerous if people have the wrong attitude.
    B completely safe if people are prepared.
    C a sport with an exciting reputation.

25 For Sam, the attraction of climbing is
    A primarily the excitement.
    B a matter of sensations.
    C hard to describe.

26 How does Sam feel when he reaches the top of a mountain?
    A proud
    B exhausted
    C amazed

27 Sam thinks that we all have a moment in childhood
    A when we know what our ambition is.
    B when we realise we can't do everything we want.
    C when we make plans about our future.

28 What was the attitude of Sam's parents when he took up the sport?
    A They were very anxious.
    B They didn't want to discourage him.
    C They gave him every support.

29 Sam explains that feeling confident
    A is the result of doing many climbs with his friend.
    B is natural after some time.
    C can provoke people to make mistakes.

30 When Sam and his friend were lost on the mountain,
    A they didn't feel lucky.
    B they thought the storm might last for a week.
    C they were sure someone would find them.

Essential tips

▸ Look closely at the questions before you hear the recording and mark the key words, including adverbs. For example, in question 24, option B uses the word *completely*. If the speaker says that the sport is *safe*, but not *completely safe*, option B is not the correct answer.

▸ If you hear a word that is in one of the options, decide whether it is used in the same way. For example, in question 25, option B includes the word *sensations*. On the recording you will hear the word *sensation*, but does that make it the correct answer?

Question 26: Questions in Part 4 ask you to interpret the speaker's feelings. It's important that you know the exact meaning of the words in the options. For instance, is *accomplished* the feeling you get when you have accomplished something?

Question 28: Words can have different meanings when used in different structures. For example, if someone is *anxious to do something*, does this mean he or she is worried?

Essential tips

Part 1

▶ Make sure you have the necessary vocabulary to give personal information. In this case, you will have to talk about the sports that you enjoy doing. You can say, for example: *I'm very keen on basketball and volleyball* or *I'm not really very interested in sports.*

▶ Listen to your partner's answer. The examiner may ask you if you agree or not.

Part 2

▶ Make sure you address both parts of the instructions. Here you will have to compare the photos but also say why you think the people are working in these different places and how they feel about working there. Give your personal opinion using expressions like *I think … , It seems to me … , In my view … , Personally, I … ,* etc.

Part 1 (2 minutes)

The examiner (interlocutor) will ask each of you to speak briefly in turn and to give personal information about yourselves. You can expect a variety of questions, such as:

What would you say are the most popular sports in your country?
Which sports do you enjoy playing? (Why?)
What kind of sports do you like watching? (Why?)
Are there any sports you find boring? (Why?)

Part 2 (4 minutes)

You will each be asked to talk for a minute without interruption. You will each be given two different photographs in turn to talk about. After your partner has finished speaking, you will be asked a brief question connected with your partner's photographs.

1 Places to work in

Look at the two photographs on page 162 which show people working in different places.

Candidate A, compare these photographs, and say why you think the people are working in these places.

Candidate B, which of these places would you prefer to work in? (Why?)

2 Family groups

Look at the two photographs on page 163 which show different family groups.

Candidate B, compare these photographs, and say what you think it would feel like to grow up in these families

Candidate A, do you think it's better to come from a small or a large family? (Why?)

Essential tips

Part 3

▸ Talk about each type of film before you reach a conclusion. Remember that there are no right or wrong answers.

▸ You are being tested on your ability to work together and complete the task. Involve your partner in the discussion using expressions like *Do you agree ... ?, What do you think ... ?, Let's decide which ... ,* etc.

▸ In deciding which type of film would appeal to students, think about students with different interests and students with different personalities. You need to justify your opinion and say why a certain type of film would appeal to the majority of the students.

Part 4

▸ Avoid giving 'yes/no' answers. Give your opinion, justify it and develop your ideas.

▸ Try to keep the conversation going by responding to your partner's answers or by asking your partner questions. You can use expressions like: *Don't you think that ... ?, How do you feel about ... ?, I agree up to a point but ... , I couldn't agree with you more, I'm sorry but I disagree with you on that,* etc.

Part 3 (4 minutes)

You will be asked to discuss something together without interruption by the examiner. You will have a page of ideas with a question to help you.

Film day

Imagine your English class is going to watch a film. Turn to page 164 which has ideas for different types of film and a question for you to discuss. Talk to each other about what type of film would appeal to students in your class. Then decide which type of film your class should watch.

Part 4 (4 minutes)

The examiner will encourage you to develop the topic of your discussion in Part 3 by asking questions such as:

What type of film do you enjoy watching? (Why?)
Do you prefer watching films at home or in the cinema? (Why? / Why not?)
Do you think watching a film in a cinema creates a special atmosphere? (Why? / Why not?)
Why do you think some films are still popular a long time after they were made?
Can you think of any recent films that will still be popular 20 or 30 years from now? (Why?)
Do you think people of different ages enjoy the same types of film? (Why? / Why not?)

PAPER 1 Reading and Use of English

▶▶ PART 5

short cut (n) a shorter way to a place than usual

envy (v) to want the same things someone else has

divert (v) to cause something or someone to change direction

give way to (phr) to be replaced by something else

haunting (adj) beautiful, but in a sad way and often in a way which cannot be forgotten

glide (v) to fly through the air without power

splashdown (n) a landing by a spacecraft, etc. in the water

picturesque (adj) like a picture, pleasing to the eye, charming

occupation (n) any activity on which you spend time

landowner (n) a person who owns land, especially undeveloped land or farmland

whereby (adv) by means of which

preserve (v) to guard, to protect from harm or change

commuter (n) a person who travels regularly, especially between home and the workplace

vital (adj) most important, absolutely necessary

lay (v) to put in place

dizzying (adj) very exciting

drop in on (phr v) to make an informal visit without an appointment

▶▶ PART 6

open-ended (adj) without limits

creativity (n) the ability to produce new things and ideas

unique (adj) different from everyone and everything else

anatomy (n) the structure of part of the body

snake (v) to move like a snake

ligament (n) what links the bones together

blood vessel (n) a tube through which blood flows in the body

fossil (n) the remains of a plant or animal that has been preserved in rock for a very long time

gene (n) part of a cell that controls a person's characteristics, passed on from parent to child

evolve (v) to develop and change over a long period of time

fin (n) part of a fish used for balance and movement

chunky (adj) small and solid

grip (v) to hold tightly

digit (n) finger

clamber (v) to move and climb with difficulty

vertebrate (n) an animal with a spine

retain (v) to keep

subtle (adj) very small

▶▶ PART 7

edition (n) a specific printing of a book or periodical

threat (n) a danger

sponsor (v) to help pay for something like a cultural or sporting event

congestion (n) excessive crowding, heavy traffic

monitor (v) to observe the actions of others

species (n) a grouping of living things

extinction (n) the act of destroying life

food chain (n) a community of organisms where each member is eaten in turn by another member

reserve (n) land kept for a special purpose

mammal (n) a warm-blooded animal, the female of which feeds its own milk to its young

launch (v) to start, to put into operation

restoration (n) making something look like it did when it was new

medieval (adj) connected with the Middle Ages (the period between about 1100 AD and 1500 AD)

PAPER 1	Reading and Use of English ▶	Part 1
		Part 2
PAPER 2	Writing	Part 3
		Part 4
PAPER 3	Listening	Part 5
PAPER 4	Speaking	Part 6
		Part 7

For questions **1–8**, read the text below and decide which word (**A, B, C** or **D**) best fits each gap. There is an example at the beginning (**0**).

Mark your answers **on the separate answer sheet**.

Example:

0	**A** awaited	**B** waited	**C** expected	**D** predicted

0	A	B	C	D
	⎽	⎽	**▬**	⎽

Vinyl attraction

Nobody ever really (**0**) …….. my Uncle Peter to make much money. When he left school, he didn't have any plans for a career, and he got a job in a second-hand record shop. Peter's mother couldn't (**1**) …….. over it. Her other children had both (**2**) …….. to get places at university, and she was quite (**3**) …….. that a young person needed a good education to get on in life. To (**4**) …….. things worse, this was the time when vinyl records were being phased out. It looked as though my uncle would soon be looking for (**5**) …….. somewhere else.

Then, all of a (**6**) …….. Peter's luck changed. He announced he was going to start collecting records and set (**7**) …….. a mail order business selling rare records. Nobody really (**8**) …….. him seriously at first. Who would be interested in a technology that's out of date? Vinyl records have since become collectors' items, and my uncle is now a very rich man.

1	**A** come	**B** take	**C** get	**D** pass
2	**A** achieved	**B** succeeded	**C** accomplished	**D** managed
3	**A** convinced	**B** persuaded	**C** determined	**D** convicted
4	**A** get	**B** make	**C** bring	**D** drive
5	**A** work	**B** job	**C** career	**D** profession
6	**A** once	**B** moment	**C** sudden	**D** minute
7	**A** up	**B** out	**C** off	**D** in
8	**A** took	**B** believed	**C** thought	**D** gave

PAPER 1	Reading and ▶	Part 1
	Use of English	Part 2
PAPER 2	Writing	Part 3
		Part 4
PAPER 3	Listening	Part 5
PAPER 4	Speaking	Part 6
		Part 7

For questions **9–16,** read the text below and think of the word which best fits each gap. Use only **one** word in each gap. There is an example at the beginning (**0**).

Write your answers **IN CAPITAL LETTERS on the separate answer sheet.**

Example: 0 W H O

Agriculture in ancient Britain

Professor Emma Thomas is an archaeologist (**0**) …….. specialises in the study of Ancient Britain and its people. The professor and her colleagues have been involved (**9**) …….. the analysis of skeletons to discover more about (**10**) …….. way Ancient Britons lived. 'Studying bones can tell us (**11**) …….. great deal about our ancestors,' says Professor Thomas. 'We know for a fact that between 9000 and 5200 BC, people ate a seafood diet, while after that people had a preference (**12**) …….. plants and animals.

(**13**) …….. is still a mystery why people gave up eating fish. One explanation might be the influence of migrants to Britain. 'Britons changed (**14**) …….. diet after people from Europe arrived,' says Professor Thomas. 'It was a time of change. Our ancestors stopped hunting and started growing crops. Farming methods (**15**) …….. imported from Europe and people no longer relied (**16**) …….. wild foods; they could control what they ate.' This marked the beginning of agriculture in Britain.

PAPER 1 Reading and ▶   Part 1
         Use of English   Part 2

PAPER 2 Writing   **Part 3**

PAPER 3 Listening   Part 4

PAPER 4 Speaking   Part 5

                 Part 6

                 Part 7

For questions **17–24,** read the text below. Use the word given in capitals at the end of some of the lines to form a word that fits in the gap **in the same line**. There is an example at the beginning (**0**).

Write your answers **IN CAPITAL LETTERS on the separate answer sheet.**

Example: **0**   A N N O U N C E M E N T

Sailing away

One Sunday morning our Aunt Emily made an (**0**)	**ANNOUNCE**
She told us (**17**) .... she was going to take us on a cruise!	**HAPPY**
I was surprised, knowing how expensive holidays like that	
were. We weren't a (**18**) .... family, but Aunt Emily said	**WEALTH**
she'd put some money aside over the years, and she	
wanted to use some of her (**19**) .... for the holiday.	**SAVE**
When the day of our (**20**) .... finally came, we were delighted	**DEPART**
and thrilled to see how huge and (**21**) .... the ship looked.	**LUXURY**
Our cruise liner sailed elegantly out to sea and our holiday	
began. But it turned out to be such a (**22**) .... !	**DISAPPOINT**
There was so little to do on the ship and we were incredibly	
bored. We visited several ports, but we didn't have the (**23**)	**FREE**
to do what we wanted. We had to follow a very tight schedule of	
guided tours and visits to museums. It was a (**24**) .... holiday!	**DISASTER**

For questions **25–30,** complete the second sentence so that it has a similar meaning to the first sentence, using the word given. **Do not change the word given.** You must use between **two** and **five** words, including the word given. Here is an example (**0**).

Example:

0   I'll be very happy when I go on holiday.

FORWARD

I'm ………………………………… on holiday.

The gap can be filled by the words 'looking forward to going' so you write:

Example: | **0** | LOOKING FORWARD TO GOING |

Write **only** the missing words **IN CAPITAL LETTERS on the separate answer sheet.**

---

25   'I'm sorry I'm late again,' he said.

APOLOGISED

He …………………………………… again.

26   She looks like my cousin Mary.

REMINDS

She …………………………………… my cousin Mary.

27   Someone is going to redecorate the kitchen for us next month.

HAVE

We are going …………………………………… next month.

28   Could you speak up because I can't hear you properly?

MIND

Would …………………………………… up because I can't hear you properly?

29   We advise customers to buy their tickets in advance.

ADVISED

Customers …………………………………… their tickets in advance.

30   It's such a pity I didn't see that film on television last night.

WISH

I …………………………………… that film on television last night.

PAPER 1 Reading and ▸   Part 1
       Use of English   Part 2

PAPER 2 Writing   Part 3
                Part 4
PAPER 3 Listening   Part 5
                Part 6
PAPER 4 Speaking   Part 7

You are going to read an article about an English poet, William Wordsworth. For questions **31–36**, choose the answer (**A**, **B**, **C** or **D**) which you think fits best according to the text.

Mark your answers **on the separate answer sheet**.

Daffodils everywhere

Two hundred years ago the English poet William Wordsworth wrote 'I wander'd lonely as a cloud', a poem that expresses a basic spirit of early English Romanticism. It was Thursday, 15 April 1802. William and Dorothy Wordsworth, the poet's devoted, journal-writing sister, were walking home to Dove Cottage in the Lake District. The wind was fierce, but the Wordsworth siblings were used to striding long distances in foul weather. They were in the woods close to the water side when they first clapped eyes on a field of daffodils 'fluttering and dancing in the breeze'.

What makes this poem an example of Romantic thinking? It isn't just that Wordsworth chooses to write about a natural scene: it is the way he describes the scene as if it had human emotions. For him, nature is not merely a neutral mixture of scenery, colours, plants, rocks, soil, water and air. It is a living force that feels joy and sadness, shares human pain and even tries to educate us human beings by showing us the beauty of life.

Wordsworth's home, Dove Cottage, is now one of the most popular destinations in the Lake District. You can go on a tour of the garden which William planted with wild flowers and which survived in his backyard even after they disappeared from the area. 'He always said that if he hadn't been a poet, he would have been a terrific landscape gardener,' says Allan King of the Wordsworth Trust, the organisation that looks after the cottage and gardens.

The Lake District in the north-west of England becomes particularly crowded during the summer months with tourists and ramblers eager to enjoy the region's majestic valleys, hills and sparkling *line 19* lakes. Wordsworth himself was far from keen on tourists, which was quite apparent. He wanted outsiders to admire the local sights he enjoyed so much, but was afraid the district might be 'damaged' by too many visitors. He opposed the coming of the trains, and campaigned in the 1840s against a plan to link the towns in the area – Kendal, Windermere and Keswick – by rail.

The place near Ullswater, where Wordsworth saw the daffodils, is at the southernmost end of the lake. The lake is wide and calm at this turning point. There's a bay where the trees have had their soil eroded by lake water so that their roots are shockingly exposed. You walk along from tree to tree, hardly daring to breathe, because you are walking in the footprints of William and Dorothy from two centuries ago. The first clumps of daffodils appear, but they aren't tall yellow trumpets proudly swaying in the breeze. They're tiny wild daffodils, most of them still green and unopened, in clumps of six or seven. They're grouped around individual trees rather than collecting together.

But as you look north, from beside a huge ancient oak, you realise this is what delighted the Wordsworths: clump after clump of the things, spread out to left and right but coming together in your vision so that they form a beautiful, pale-yellow carpet. What you're seeing at last is nature transformed by human sight and imagination. For a second, you share that revelation of Dorothy and William Wordsworth's, the glimpse of pantheism, the central mystery of English Romanticism.

31 According to the article, Wordsworth's poem

    A   started the Romantic movement.
    B   was based on actual experience.
    C   was written while he was visiting his sister.
    D   was written after he had been lonely.

32 What was Wordsworth's attitude to nature?

    A   He believed nature had a character of its own.
    B   He felt nature was human.
    C   He thought nature could talk to people.
    D   He believed that we could influence nature.

33 We are told that Dove Cottage

    A   has gardens designed by a landscape gardener.
    B   has a wide range of flowers in its garden.
    C   receives a lot of visitors.
    D   has a very large garden.

34 What does 'which' in line 19 refer to?

    A   the number of tourists who come to the Lake District
    B   Wordsworth's desire for outsiders to admire the local sights
    C   the fact that Wordsworth was keen on tourists from far away
    D   Wordsworth's dislike of tourists

35 In what way is the scene different from what Wordsworth described?

    A   All the daffodils are green and small.
    B   There are no daffodils by the lake.
    C   The daffodils are fewer and smaller.
    D   There are no daffodils around trees.

36 The writer implies that the poem describes

    A   exactly what Wordsworth saw in detail.
    B   the effect the daffodils had on Wordsworth.
    C   what Wordsworth saw around an ancient oak.
    D   clumps of daffodils on the left and on the right.

PAPER 1	Reading and ▸	Part 1
	Use of English	Part 2
PAPER 2	Writing	Part 3
		Part 4
PAPER 3	Listening	Part 5
PAPER 4	Speaking	**Part 6**
		Part 7

You are going to read a newspaper article about the benefits of playing computer games. Six sentences have been removed from the article. Choose from the sentences **A–G** the one which fits each gap (**37–42**). There is one extra sentence, which you do not need to use.

Mark your answers **on the separate answer sheet**.

Computer games: not just for kids!

More people than ever are turning to computer games for fun and health benefits

Susie Bullen lines up, swings her arm back, and releases another perfect throw for yet another strike. When the game is over, the 94-year-old has rolled a personal best of 220. But Bullen isn't hanging out in the local bowling alley – she's playing on a popular interactive gaming system that has gained immense popularity with people of all ages.

Bullen, who once competed in leagues but hasn't bowled in nearly 70 years, said the interactive sports games give her the opportunity to reconnect to many of the activities she enjoyed in her formative years. 'I try to play as much as I can,' says Bullen, resident of a peaceful retirement community in Ontario, Canada. **37** Bullen regularly competes against her great-granddaughter, 16-year-old Melanie, on her gaming console.

Bullen is amongst a growing number of older people participating in this kind of pastime, which is helping to bring generations together in a shared activity. 'It's great fun playing against my great-grandma', says Melanie. **38**

According to recent research in the entertainment software sector, the percentage of people over 50 playing computer games has more than doubled since the year 2000, and the number is expected to increase as the popularity and visibility of current computer game platforms continue to grow. **39**

Interactive games have been linked to providing increased mental and physical well-being across the age groups. In addition to boosting mood, playing an 'exer-game' for around half an hour, three times a week, improves balance and leaves players feeling refreshed and energised. **40** Just like traditional forms of exercise, interactive gaming promotes better mental sharpness and hand-eye coordination. And one study has shown that there are some characteristics of gaming that promote visual learning, too – that is, acquiring skills through associating ideas and concepts with images and techniques.

So, what is it that has attracted older people to join in the gaming world? **41** Not only are the most successful platforms those with user-friendly controls, but the best games for the whole family to get involved in together are those which aren't overly-complicated, but still offer plenty in terms of stimulus.

42 A ten-pin bowling game, for example, requires users to swing their arms in the same motion as a bowler, while holding down a button on the controller. When the player is ready to release the ball, he or she simply releases the button. And as he or she does so, the feel-good factor is released along with it!

A In a market flooded with thousands and thousands of games, finding the right fit can be challenging.

B And as computer game usage amongst older people has risen, researchers have conducted studies that have concluded that computer games provide much more than simple entertainment value.

C 'I've always been sports-minded and like watching sports. Playing computer games is a bit of fun and it's great to see how you can do, as well as providing some much-needed exercise.'

D Games which mimic the movements of the sports they represent are particularly popular amongst gamers who not only want to have fun, but want to incorporate a bit of heart-pumping action into their free-time activities as well.

E This includes balance boards that record movements and give feedback on performance. Activities include yoga poses, push-ups, strength, balance and aerobic exercises.

F 'She's a real pro and it's hard for me to keep up! She's a fantastic opponent and we have a lot of laughs.'

G Active game-playing helps people of all ages recognise that exercise can be fun and socially enjoyable, and isn't just about hitting the treadmill at the gym.

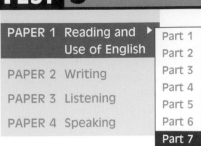
PAPER 1	Reading and ▶	Part 1
	Use of English	Part 2
PAPER 2	Writing	Part 3
		Part 4
PAPER 3	Listening	Part 5
PAPER 4	Speaking	Part 6
		Part 7

You are going to read a magazine article about people who work from home. For questions **43–52**, choose from the people (**A–D**). The people may be chosen more than once.

Mark your answers **on the separate answer sheet.**

Which person

is aware of the importance of conforming to industry requirements? **43** ☐

understands the health implications of certain types of work? **44** ☐

compares two different places of work? **45** ☐

mentions a natural phenomenon that helps her concentrate? **46** ☐

doesn't think she would take as much pleasure in her work in a different place? **47** ☐

appreciates the need to feel mentally and physically prepared for work? **48** ☐

recognises that her current workplace benefits others as well as herself? **49** ☐

has improved her efficiency by adapting her workplace to her needs? **50** ☐

has observed a particular effect of where she works on what she creates? **51** ☐

is grateful that she is able to leave work behind when she's finished for the day? **52** ☐

Working from home

A Petra Rosso

I'm a student, which means I have to have peace and solitude when I'm trying to get my assignments done for college. There's a great attic room at home which I've been working in. I'm studying creative writing and it's important not only to get into the right frame of mind, but the right surroundings, too, in order for the ideas to flow. The room's flooded with light which helps me stay really focused when I'm writing, and the view from the window is inspiring. In fact, I've done some of my best work since I've been using the room for study purposes. The benefits extend beyond the walls of the room too – once the door's closed, it means I can totally switch off and spend time with my family without the thought of college work interfering.

B Jade Pickett

I share a large apartment with some other young professionals like myself. We get on well together and tend to congregate in the kitchen, which is large and spacious. I like to keep it clean and tidy as I run a catering business from home and it's imperative that I stick to certain standards of cleanliness. I'm always experimenting with new dishes and often prepare meals for my flatmates and our friends who come over. What could be more fun than chilling out with good company and food? I like the sociable atmosphere that cooking can create and without such a lovely space to try things out in, I doubt I'd enjoy what I do even half as much.

C Kara Francis

As an artist, it's vital to have the right working environment. I do have a room at home designated for the purpose, though it's undergoing a bit of renovation work at the moment, so I'm working in the living room for the time being. It's a light, airy space and there are some huge glass doors leading out onto the back of the house, which looks over the fields. It's almost like the countryside spills into the house. I paint portraits and the light there makes it almost as good as working in my studio. The people who sit for me can look out at the greenery while I'm studying them, and it's fascinating what a calming effect this seems to have on them. I've noticed recently that the portraits I've produced lately have a real air of serenity about them.

D Tina Tyford

I work from home and have a home office, which is the ideal place to get my head down and run my business. When I first started working from home, I undertook some research into what makes the best environment for home-workers and that included buying some ergonomic furniture which I had specially designed to suit my needs. Yes, the financial outlay was significant, but it's really increased my performance and output. I know that having a sedentary job can cause physical problems, so making sure I have the right chair to support my back and so on makes an enormous difference. My office is also well lit and all necessary equipment is within easy reach of my desk. It was definitely worth the effort I put in to make the room suitable for my requirements.

PAPER 1 Reading and
Use of English

PAPER 2 Writing ▶ Part 1
Part 2

PAPER 3 Listening

PAPER 4 Speaking

You **must** answer this question. Write your answer in **140–190** words in an appropriate style.

1 In your English class you have been comparing using public transport with travelling by car. Now, your teacher has asked you to write an essay.

Write an essay using **all** the notes and give reasons for your point of view.

Do you think it is better to use public transport than travel by car?

Notes
Write about:

1. environmental effects
2. cost
3. .... (your own idea)

Write an answer to **one** of the questions **2–5** in this part. Write your answer in **140–190** words in an appropriate style.

2   You have seen this announcement in a magazine called *Sports World Monthly.*

> **SPORTS WORLD MONTHLY**
>
> What is your favourite sport? What kind of clothes and equipment do you need for this sport? Does this sport require any special qualities?
>
> We will publish the best article.

Write your **article**.

3   This is part of a letter you have received from Sam, your English-speaking friend.

> In class we've been talking about how the places we live in change. Can you tell me about how your neighbourhood has changed? Do you think the changes are positive or negative?
>
> See you soon!
>
> Sam

Write your **letter**.

4   You have recently used a good website where you can download music. Write a review of the website for your student magazine. Include information about how the website is better than others of its type, and say what the special features of the website are. Say who you would recommend the website for.

Write your **review**.

5   (*for FIRST FOR SCHOOLS candidates only*)

Answer the following question based on your reading of **one** of the set books.

'A good book always conveys an important message.' Your teacher has asked you to write an **essay**, giving your opinions on this statement with reference to the book or one of the short stories you have read.

PAPER 1 Reading and
Use of English

PAPER 2 Writing

PAPER 3 Listening ▶ Part 1
                       Part 2
                       Part 3
                       Part 4

PAPER 4 Speaking

Track 9

You will hear people talking in eight different situations. For questions **1–8**, choose the best answer (**A**, **B** or **C**).

1   You hear a man talking about planting flower seeds in his garden.
    When does he expect them to grow?
    A   June
    B   May
    C   April

2   You hear two friends talking about when they last met.
    What was the occasion?
    A   a birthday party
    B   a wedding
    C   a Christmas party

3   You hear a woman talking about the kind of book she currently enjoys reading.
    What kind of book is it?
    A   romance
    B   detective novel
    C   fairytale

4   You hear two friends discussing the sports they play.
    Which sport do they most enjoy playing?
    A   basketball
    B   tennis
    C   volleyball

5   You hear a shop assistant talking to a customer.
    What is the customer looking for?
    A   a shirt
    B   a suit
    C   a sweater

6   You hear a man talking about his job as a lighting technician in a theatre.
    How does he feel about tonight's performance?
    A   concerned about making mistakes
    B   surprised to be so nervous about the experience
    C   excited about working in live theatre

7   You hear a boy talking about school.
    Which subject does he like best?
    A   maths
    B   art
    C   history

8   You hear a travel agent talking about a journey.
    What is the customer's final destination?
    A   Houston
    B   New York
    C   Los Angeles

🎧 **Track 10**

You will hear a man called Tom Botham giving a talk about newspaper journalism.
For questions **9–18**, complete the sentences with a word or short phrase.

Journalism

Tom mentions business, news, sport and (**9**) ....

as examples of what journalists write about.

Many journalists have a degree in journalism, though Tom took his in

(**10**) ....

Tom says it's important to gain a certificate in reporting, carrying out

(**11**) .... and editing.

When applying for a job, Tom says you need to show a selection of

(**12**) .... you've written.

Tom got experience of writing by working as a (**13**) ....

on a student magazine.

Tom says journalists must have good communication and

(**14**) .... skills, in addition to personal characteristics

such as motivation.

Tom was able to demonstrate to employers his experience of

(**15**) ....

As a junior reporter, Tom was pleased to attend

(**16**) .... as well as other local events.

In Tom's present job, he has a range of responsibilities and most enjoys doing

(**17**) ....

Tom is currently exploring the idea of working as a

(**18**) .... on the paper.

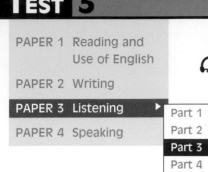

PAPER 1 Reading and
Use of English

PAPER 2 Writing

PAPER 3 Listening ▶

PAPER 4 Speaking

Part 1
Part 2
Part 3
Part 4

🎧 **Track 11**

You will hear five short extracts in which people are talking about their favourite films. For questions **19–23**, choose from the list (**A–H**) the reason each speaker gives for his or her preference. Use the letters only once. There are three extra letters which you do not need to use.

A It has a complex storyline.

B You want to know what happens next.

C It is highly amusing.

D It has an unexpected ending.

E It is very true to life.

F The special effects are interesting.

G The acting is outstanding.

H It has an unusual theme.

Speaker 1 | **19**

Speaker 2 | **20**

Speaker 3 | **21**

Speaker 4 | **22**

Speaker 5 | **23**

Track 12

You will hear part of a radio interview with a woman called Alice Barker, who has a rare condition called synaesthesia. For questions **24–30**, choose the best answer (**A**, **B** or **C**).

24 Alice describes her ability as
    A   connecting emotions and words.
    B   linking colours and emotions.
    C   connecting colours with words.

25 We are told that Alice developed this condition
    A   because it is in her family.
    B   when she was a child.
    C   when she had children.

26 When she was younger, Alice and her brother
    A   used to think they were going mad.
    B   would argue about the colours connected with words.
    C   saw the same colours for certain words.

27 Alice says that this ability
    A   is directly associated with her moods.
    B   can make her feel depressed.
    C   makes her feelings more intense.

28 What is the effect of Alice's condition on her reading?
    A   It makes her read more descriptions of colours.
    B   It can encourage her to reread a sentence.
    C   It makes her avoid sentences with bright descriptions.

29 Alice feels that having this condition
    A   is very unpleasant at times.
    B   is generally not a problem.
    C   is not pleasant at all, on the whole.

30 Doctors used to believe that this condition
    A   made people insane.
    B   only affected the insane.
    C   indicated the person was going mad.

Part 1 (2 minutes)

The examiner (interlocutor) will ask each of you to speak briefly in turn and to give personal information about yourselves. You can expect a variety of questions, such as:

When did you start learning English?
In what ways do you think English is going to be useful for you?
Do you have any plans for a future career?
Will you be able to use foreign languages in the career you choose?

Part 2 (4 minutes)

You will each be asked to talk for a minute without interruption. You will each be given two different photographs in turn to talk about. After your partner has finished speaking, you will be asked a brief question connected with your partner's photographs.

> **1 Meals**

Look at the two photographs on page 165 which show people having different sorts of meals.

Candidate A, compare these photographs, and say how you think the people feel in these situations.

Candidate B, which of these sorts of meals would you enjoy most? (Why?)

> **2 Cars**

Look at the two photographs on page 166 which show different cars.

Candidate B, compare these photographs, and say how you think it would feel to travel in these cars.

Candidate A, which of these cars would you prefer to travel in? (Why?)

Part 3 (4 minutes)

You will be asked to discuss something together without interruption by the examiner. You will have a page of ideas and a question to help you.

> **Outdoor activities**

Imagine you are helping to organise an outdoor activity holiday for a group of teenagers. Turn to page 167 which has ideas for activities and a question for you to discuss. Talk to each other about the advantages and disadvantages of these outdoor activities. Then decide which two activities should be chosen.

Part 4 (4 minutes)

The examiner will encourage you to develop the topic of your discussion in Part 3 by asking questions such as:

What are the most popular sports to watch and play in your country?
Do you prefer team sports or individual sports? (Why?)
What skills do team sports require? (Why?)
Why do you think some people are good at sports and others aren't?
Do you think some sports are too expensive to play? (Why? / Why not?)
Do you think professional sportspeople earn too much money? (Why? / Why not?)

PAPER 1 Reading and Use of English

▸▸ **PART 5**

devoted (adj) giving someone a lot of love and attention

fierce (adj) powerful, intense

sibling (n) a brother or sister

stride (v) to walk strongly with long steps

foul (adj) foul weather is stormy and windy, with rain or snow

clap eyes on someone/something (phr) to see someone/something, especially when you did not expect to

flutter (v) to wave very quickly and lightly

breeze (n) a gentle wind

neutral (adj) neutral language deliberately avoids expressing strong feelings

landscape gardener (n) a skilled worker who designs and works on landscaped areas

rambler (n) someone who goes for long walks for enjoyment

eager (adj) keen and excited

far from (phr) used to say that something different is true

campaign (v) to try to achieve something by persuading people or the government to do something

erode (v) to wear away, to wash away

exposed (adj) not covered

clump (n) a group, mass, or cluster

sway (v) to move back and forth, to rock

transform (v) to change from one shape or appearance to another

revelation (n) an uncovering of something that was hidden, a disclosure

▸▸ **PART 6**

turn to (v) to start doing something new or different

hang out (v) to spend time somewhere

formative (adj) relating to a period of early development

visibility (n) the capability of being easily observed

platform (n) hardware or software that can be accessed online

well-being (n) when someone is happy, healthy and comfortable

boost (v) to improve or increase something

energise (v) to give energy to

mental sharpness (n) the ability to notice and understand things

hand-eye coordination (n) the coordinated control of hand movement with eye movement

stimulus (n) something that makes something else happen, grow or develop more

flood (v) to enter or fill a place in large numbers or amounts

mimic (v) to copy or imitate closely

incorporate (v) to include something as part of another thing

opponent (n) a person who takes the opposite side in a fight, game, contest, etc.

hit (v) to go to

▸▸ **PART 7**

solitude (n) being alone

attic (n) a space in a house, just under the roof

frame of mind (n) the way someone feels at a particular time

flow (v) to move in a smooth, continuous way

extend (v) to continue

switch off (v) relax

interfere (v) to intrude

congregate (v) to gather together

spacious (adj) large, with plenty of room

catering (n) providing food and drink for people

imperative (adj) essential

chill out (v) to relax

vital (adj) essential

designate (v) to set aside for a purpose

renovation (n) the act of repairing and redecorating

serenity (n) a feeling of calmness and happiness

get your head down (v) to direct all your efforts to a particular task

undertake (v) to do something, to carry something out

ergonomic (adj) designed to create maximum comfort

outlay (n) cost

output (n) an amount of something produced by a person

sedentary (adj) spending a lot of time sitting down

For questions **1–8**, read the text below and decide which word (**A**, **B**, **C** or **D**) best fits each gap. There is an example at the beginning (**0**).

Mark your answers **on the separate answer sheet**.

Example:

0 **A** informed   **B** told   **C** shown   **D** said

0	A	B	C	D

School lunch

Research has (**0**) .... that over half the children in Britain who take their own lunches to school do not eat properly in the middle of the day. In Britain schools have to provide meals at lunchtime. Children can (**1**) .... to bring their own food or have lunch in the school canteen.

One surprising (**2**) .... of this research is that school meals are much healthier than lunches brought in from home. There are strict standards for the preparation of school meals, which have to include fruit, vegetables, meat and a dairy item. Lunchboxes (**3**) .... by researchers contained sweet drinks, crisps and chocolate bars, so the children (**4**) .... an unhealthy amount of sugar at lunchtime.

The research will provide a better (**5**) .... of why the percentage of overweight students in Britain has (**6**) .... in the last decade. Children can easily develop bad eating (**7**) .... at this age, and it's important to try and do something to (**8**) .... it.

1	**A** prefer	**B** manage	**C** want	**D** choose
2	**A** finding	**B** number	**C** figure	**D** factor
3	**A** examined	**B** found	**C** taken	**D** looked
4	**A** take	**B** contain	**C** consume	**D** consist
5	**A** view	**B** knowledge	**C** understanding	**D** opinion
6	**A** expanded	**B** increased	**C** extended	**D** added
7	**A** customs	**B** styles	**C** attitudes	**D** habits
8	**A** prevent	**B** define	**C** decide	**D** delay

For questions **9–16**, read the text below and think of the word which best fits each gap. Use only **one** word in each gap. There is an example at the beginning (**0**).

Write your answers **IN CAPITAL LETTERS on the separate answer sheet**.

Example: | 0 | T H E R E | | | | | | | | | | | | | | | | |

History and storytelling

Over the last few years (**0**) …….. has been more interest in the subject of history, perhaps because historical documentaries on television have (**9**) …….. attracting large audiences. According to a recent survey, more people are applying (**10**) …….. places at university, and the number of those wanting to study history (**11**) …….. increased. However, professors of history are (**12**) …….. particularly happy about this and have expressed concern about the quality of their students. They claim that most of their first-year students have never read a history book and don't have the skills (**13**) …….. study the subject in depth. TV programmes make students think that studying history is as simple as storytelling. Documentaries oversimplify the subject and concentrate (**14**) …….. personalities in an attempt to attract audiences.

On the other hand, traditional historians could learn (**15**) …….. to tell a story from the makers of such documentaries. Many historians don't have good narrative skills, which is (**16**) …….. so many history books are not popular with readers.

For questions **17–24**, read the text below. Use the word given in capitals at the end of some of the lines to form a word that fits in the gap **in the same line**. There is an example at the beginning (**0**).

Write your answers **IN CAPITAL LETTERS on the separate answer sheet**.

Example: ⟨0⟩ ⟨D⟩⟨A⟩⟨N⟩⟨G⟩⟨E⟩⟨R⟩⟨O⟩⟨U⟩⟨S⟩ ⟨⟩⟨⟩⟨⟩⟨⟩⟨⟩⟨⟩⟨⟩

Diving deeper

Free-diving is an extremely (**0**) .... sport, which is perhaps   **DANGER**
why its (**17**) .... has grown so fast. Free-divers are attached   **POPULAR**
to a line, and then they have to take a deep breath, dive as
deep as they can and come up (**18**) ....   **IMMEDIATE**

The British free-diver, Tanya Streeter, trains very (**19**) ....   **CARE**
before each dive to build up her physical (**20**) .... She never   **FIT**
dives until she's completely confident that she's ready.

'The danger is caused by the great (**21**) .... at those depths.   **PRESS**
I think that safety procedures have to be very strict if we
want to avoid accidents,' Tanya says. Tanya feels that mental
strength is also very important. She has an emotional response
to water and feels very calm when she's underwater. Perhaps
Tanya's greatest asset is her (**22**) .... to focus. 'In free-diving   **ABLE**
there are no (**23**) .... around you and there are no cheering   **COMPETE**
spectators to (**24**) .... you. It's a lonely sport,' says Tanya.   **COURAGE**

PAPER 1	Reading and Use of English ▸	Part 1
		Part 2
PAPER 2	Writing	Part 3
		Part 4
PAPER 3	Listening	Part 5
		Part 6
PAPER 4	Speaking	Part 7

For questions **25–30,** complete the second sentence so that it has a similar meaning to the first sentence, using the word given. **Do not change the word given.** You must use between **two** and **five** words, including the word given. Here is an example (**0**).

Example:

0 I'll be very happy when I go on holiday.

FORWARD

I'm .... on holiday.

The gap can be filled by the words 'looking forward to going' so you write:

Example: | **0** | LOOKING FORWARD TO GOING |

Write only the missing words **IN CAPITAL LETTERS on the separate answer sheet**.

---

25 The basketball coach will make me train very hard.

MADE

I .... very hard by the basketball coach.

26 'You can watch if you keep quiet,' said the actor.

PROVIDED

The actor said that I could watch .... quiet.

27 I regret not telling you the whole truth.

TOLD

I wish .... the whole truth.

28 After hours of negotiation, they managed to get the new contract.

SUCCEEDED

After hours of negotiation, they .... the new contract.

29 She tried to stay cheerful although she felt sick.

SPITE

She tried to stay cheerful .... sick.

30 Mike probably won't come to the party.

UNLIKELY

Mike .... to the party.

PAPER 1 Reading and
         Use of English

PAPER 2 Writing

PAPER 3 Listening

PAPER 4 Speaking

Part 1
Part 2
Part 3
Part 4
Part 5
Part 6
Part 7

You are going to read an article about noise. For questions **31–36**, choose the answer (**A**, **B**, **C** or **D**) which you think fits best according to the text.

Mark your answers **on the separate answer sheet**.

Noise: traveller's enemy or traveller's friend?

'Passport, boarding pass, phone…' As my taxi zips towards the airport, suddenly a cord of panic pulls tight around my chest. I thrust my hand into one compartment of my handbag, then another. It's not anywhere. My mouth opens, and the words, 'Driver, turn around! Now!' almost spring out. But I swallow them. We're halfway to the airport, and I'm already running late. Surely I can survive one trip without my supply of foam earplugs?

I'm a generally good traveller except for one thing that undoes me every time: noise. Ask me about my absolute worst travel experiences, and I'll tell you the story about that night I spent in a cheap hotel that also happens to be the venue for the most popular Saturday night disco in the area. Elsewhere, there were the chickens that always began crowing at 2 a.m. at a rural retreat (no one, I guess, informed them that they shouldn't get going until dawn). And there was also the deeply discounted hotel room with 'swimming pool view' that I was so pleased with myself for finding. The swimming pool, it turned out, was under renovation. Actively. With power drills. Directly below my window.

In my ideal traveller's world I'd control the volume of everything, like a music producer at a giant mixing board. There would be no blasting television sets hanging above public squares or embedded in taxi seats, no cheesy songs playing in the shops. Loud noise would be completely absent. Everywhere. But no traveller can remain in a perfectly controlled sonic bubble. Not when we're moving through a world in which what constitutes noise has so many different interpretations, including whether noise is ever a bad thing. For sound is relative: one person's noise is another person's music, or expression of happiness.

On one of the first extended trips I ever took, I travelled to an island for Carnival, which is basically like deciding to pitch your tent inside a dance hall for three weeks. At any hour, different kinds of music would float through the air and, without warning, straight into my ear. Neighbours shouted to each other over the din, then turned up the volume on their radios. It was a non-stop celebration, during which I got very little sleep. It was fabulous. The thing is, the noise that wraps a city in Carnival happiness is more than just noise: it's the sound of a human community. To block it out is to risk missing something really fundamental about a place – and the reassuring feeling of being part of something larger than yourself. Noise brings people together. I've learnt this over and over in my travels, but it hasn't been an easy lesson to accept.

line 24

I struggle against my instinct to isolate myself in a cocoon of silence. I really don't want to cut myself off from the thrill of human noise. But I don't want to go crazy, either. Nowadays, unwanted – and largely non-human – sounds push and shove travellers from all directions. Cars, subways, construction, jet engines: their clamour seems omnipresent. Yet instead of lowering the volume of everyday living, we seem to layer noise upon noise. The hotel bar jacks up its techno music to counteract the babble in the lobby. The traveller walking along traffic-choked streets retreats into her iPod.

On the plane, I press my foam earplug deep into my ear. As it slowly expands to fill my ear canal, I savour the journey into the bliss of noiselessness. Thank goodness the convenience store at the airport stocks one of travel's most essential items. The headache-inducing whine of the jet engines magically fades away, and I'm once again the master of my private sonic world. To appreciate the comfort of noise, you also need the comfort of silence. I'll unplug when I get to where I'm going.

31 What is the writer doing in the first paragraph?

    A demonstrating how well organised she is
    B explaining why she is in a particular situation
    C describing something that often happens to her
    D showing how important something is to her

32 What do the writer's worst travel experiences tell us about her?

    A She is annoyed when the facilities advertised are not available.
    B She is willing to stay in places that are not particularly luxurious.
    C She tries to plan ahead in order to avoid certain situations.
    D She finds unusual locations especially attractive.

33 What does the writer say about her 'ideal traveller's world'?

    A She realises it isn't actually the best way to travel.
    B She wishes she didn't have to share it with others.
    C She travels in the hope of finding it one day.
    D She knows other people wouldn't like it.

34 What does 'It' refer to in line 24?

    A getting very little sleep
    B the volume on people's radios
    C the non-stop celebration
    D the neighbours shouting

35 What does the writer say about noise in the fifth paragraph?

    A People are born with a need to hear it.
    B People deal with it by creating more of it.
    C It affects people in a number of different ways.
    D Modern life offers effective protection from it.

36 How does the writer feel in the final paragraph?

    A relieved she will not have to hear any noise at her destination
    B grateful to know she can find earplugs wherever she goes
    C pleased she can decide for herself whether to hear things or not
    D glad to be able to choose what music she'll listen to on the flight

PAPER 1	Reading and	▶	Part 1
	Use of English		Part 2
PAPER 2	Writing		Part 3
			Part 4
PAPER 3	Listening		Part 5
PAPER 4	Speaking		Part 6
			Part 7

You are going to read an article about an expedition to look at a mountain under the sea. Six sentences have been removed from the article. Choose from the sentences **A–G** the one which fits each gap (**37–42**). There is one extra sentence, which you do not need to use.

Mark your answers **on the separate answer sheet**.

Mountains in the sea

An ocean scientist visits a mountain, or 'seamount', deep under the ocean.

Sealed in our special deep-sea sphere, we wait until we are untied, drifting, a tiny dot on the immense Pacific Ocean. Then we sink into the water, surrounded by bubbles. A diver pokes through the bubbles to make a final adjustment to the camera mounted on the outside of the submersible sphere (known as a 'sub'). Out there with the camera are hydraulics, thrusters, and hundreds of other essential parts that will keep us safe.

Three of us are crammed inside a sphere 1.5 metres in diameter, surrounded by communication equipment, controls, snacks, cameras. **37** Its peaks, rarely seen up close before, rise from the bottom of the Pacific near Cocos Island. The highest peak here is more than 2,200 metres tall.

Seamounts generally form when volcanic mountains rise up from the sea floor but fail to reach the surface (those that break the surface become islands). Scientists estimate that there are some 100,000 seamounts at least one kilometre high. But if you include others that range from small hills to rolling mountains, there may be as many as a million of them. We've seen little of these oases of life in the deep. Of all earth's seamounts, marine biologists have studied only a few hundred. **38**

Scientists don't often explore their slopes first hand – or even their shallower summits: living mazes of hard coral, sponges and sea fans circled by schools of fish. **39** Among this abundance of sea creatures, might there be new species that could produce new chemical compounds that can cure diseases?

Unfortunately, more and more frequently deep-sea fishing trawlers drag nets weighted with heavy chains across seamounts to catch schools of fish that congregate around them. **40** Once these underwater communities are disrupted, it can take hundreds, even thousands, of years for them to re-establish themselves.

We turn a ghostly greenish blue in the light, kept dim so we can see outside. Clear, pulsing jellies glide gently in the dark, bouncing off the sub in every direction. A black-and-white manta ray flexes its wings and soars past for a look. We are still in what is called the photic zone, where sunlight penetrates and provides energy for countless microscopic, photosynthetic ocean plants that create much of the earth's oxygen. **41**

At about 200 metres the sub's dazzling lights bring the bottom into view. **42** We joke that maybe we've found a new wreck, but instead it is the remains of a volcano, perhaps millions of years old. Within minutes the sub is hovering a few centimetres from the bottom, inside an ancient, circular vent of the now extinct volcano that forms Las Gemelas. Its sculptured walls look like the facade of a deep-sea cathedral.

Our sub surfaces after five hours – all too soon. We begin the long journey back to our land-based lives, where we will analyse our data and add one more piece to the puzzle of our global ocean.

A This process also destroys long-lived and slow-growing corals, sponges, and other invertebrates.

B These under-sea mountains have therefore been well known for a number of years.

C Then we descend further, and the ocean around us is completely black.

D More finely detailed maps of the surface of Mars may exist than of the remotest parts of the ocean floor.

E Suddenly something just beyond them rises from the otherwise featureless sea floor.

F We have everything we need for our journey to reach a seamount named Las Gemelas.

G Some of these animals have even lived to be more than a hundred years old.

PAPER 1 Reading and ▶
          Use of English
PAPER 2 Writing
PAPER 3 Listening
PAPER 4 Speaking

Part 1
Part 2
Part 3
Part 4
Part 5
Part 6
Part 7

You are going to read an article in which four young people talk about the experience of taking their driving test. For questions **43–52**, choose from the people (**A–D**). The people may be chosen more than once.

Mark your answers **on the separate answer sheet**.

Which person

failed the driving test three times?	**43**
thought learning to drive would be easier than it was?	**44**
was discouraged from driving by a relative?	**45**
was very nervous at first?	**46**
is going to drive a vehicle at work?	**47**
practised driving on private land?	**48**
nearly missed the test?	**49**
hasn't driven since taking the test?	**50**
will soon own a car?	**51**
could previously use another type of vehicle?	**52**

First steps at driving

How do young people feel about learning to drive?
We asked four youngsters who have recently passed the test.

A Joe Smedley

I used to make models of cars, and I knew a lot about different makes long before I was old enough to drive one. I'd been riding a motorbike for six months before I started taking lessons for my driving test, and I'm sure that experience helped me. On the other hand, learning to drive proved to be quite hard. I thought because I knew how a car works it would make a difference. That was a big mistake! I remember how embarrassed I was when I couldn't even get the car into second gear. By the time I took my test, I felt fairly confident, so I wasn't surprised when I passed first time. The funny thing about it is that I haven't had the chance to drive a car ever since I got my licence because my parents don't have one!

B Hanna Watson

I'm really glad that I have a driving licence because it's so useful, but I wasn't really sure I wanted to take the test at first. I was shaking and my knees were trembling before the first lesson, though I felt better because the instructor was so friendly. Although he assured me I was ready to take the test after 25 lessons, I decided to wait until I had had a few more. I felt very tense about driving, and the test was a disaster. First, I forgot my glasses when I went for the written test, and then, on the practical test, I got there five minutes' late because the bus I was on broke down! It wasn't my fault, and luckily they let me go ahead with it anyway, but I was quite upset. Anyway, for the last few months I've been practising in my father's car, although he only lets me go on quiet country roads.

C Clarissa Holmes

I wanted to get my driving licence as soon as I could. My childhood ambition was to be the first woman Formula One world champion! Actually, the reality of taking my test was completely different from what I'd expected. I didn't pass the test until my fourth attempt, but that was because of the practical test. I kept on making silly mistakes, you see. In fact, the other part of the test wasn't nearly as hard; all you had to do was learn the regulations about driving.

I was getting pretty upset after failing three times, so my aunt, who owns a farm, let me go into a field and drive around, just to get used to the feeling. I think that helped a lot. I've been saving up like mad, and in a couple of weeks I'm confident I'll have enough to buy a decent second-hand car.

D Eddy Fredricks

I didn't really think about taking my driving test right up until I was 18. I had the idea that driving was basically dangerous, and I think that came from my grandmother. She had never got used to driving in busy traffic, and she used to tell me how awful it was, which put me off a lot. But when a couple of my friends passed their tests, I suddenly realised I really wanted to get my driving licence.

Being optimistic, I just booked ten lessons at first, but in the end I needed over three times that many! Having a driving licence is going to be very useful. When the school term finishes in August, I've got a part-time job delivering books for a big bookshop, and I have to use their delivery van, so I couldn't do it if I hadn't passed my test.

You **must** answer this question. Write your answer in **140–190** words in an appropriate style.

1 In your English class you have been talking about sport. Now, your English teacher has asked you to write an essay for homework.

Write an essay using **all** the notes and giving reasons for your point of view.

Is playing a team sport the best way to get fit?

Notes
Write about:

1. exercising with other people
2. how convenient it is
3. .... (your own idea)

PAPER 1 Reading and
Use of English

PAPER 2 Writing ▶ Part 1
Part 2

PAPER 3 Listening

PAPER 4 Speaking

Write an answer to **one** of the questions **2–5** in this part. Write your answer in **140–190** words in an appropriate style.

___

2 You see this announcement on an English-language website.

> ### Articles wanted!
> ### Music
>
> How important is music in your life?
>
> What sort of music do you enjoy? Why?
>
> Who do you listen to it with?
>
> Write us an article answering these questions. The best articles will be posted on the website.

Write your **article**.

3 You recently saw a film about a famous historical event in your country. Write a review of the film for your college magazine. Include information about the story, the characters and costumes, and say whether the film was historically accurate.

Write your **review**.

4 (*for FIRST candidates only*)

Your teacher has asked you to write a report about the eating habits of young people in your area. Describe what most young people eat and suggest how they could be encouraged to eat healthier food.

Write your **report**.

(*for FIRST FOR SCHOOLS candidates only*)

You see this announcement in an international magazine for young people.

> ### Stories wanted
>
> We are looking for stories for our magazine. Your story must begin with this sentence:
>
> *Helen and Steve looked at each other and burst out laughing.*
>
> Your story must include:
> * a photograph
> * a computer

Write your **story**.

5 (*for FIRST FOR SCHOOLS candidates only*)

Answer the following question based on your reading of one of the set books.

Write an **essay** describing an event in the book or short story you have read which plays a main role in the development of the plot and affects the characters.

PAPER 1   Reading and
            Use of English

PAPER 2   Writing

PAPER 3   Listening   ▶ | Part 1 |
                               | Part 2 |
PAPER 4   Speaking | Part 3 |
                               | Part 4 |

🎧 **Track 13**

You will hear people talking in eight different situations. For questions **1–8**, choose the best answer (**A**, **B** or **C**).

---

1   You hear a woman bringing an MP3 player back to the shop where she bought it.
        What is the problem with it?
        A   It plays tracks at the wrong speed.
        B   It jumps from one track to the next.
        C   It doesn't switch off properly.

2   You hear a woman talking to a waiter.
        What does she want him to bring her?
        A   mineral water
        B   coffee
        C   orange juice

3   You hear a man describing a journey.
        Where did he want to go?
        A   Leeds
        B   Manchester
        C   Crewe

4   You hear an advertisement for a sale in a furniture store.
        Which items have the biggest reductions?
        A   sofas
        B   beds
        C   armchairs

5   You hear a woman talking to a car mechanic.
        What is the problem with her car?
        A   It won't start in wet weather.
        B   The brakes don't work properly.
        C   The engine keeps on stopping.

6   You hear a graphic designer talking about his work.
        How does he feel about the recent change in his job?
        A   He thinks his new work is boring.
        B   He regrets giving up his previous job.
        C   He thinks he's made the right decision.

7   You hear a radio announcement about traffic on a motorway.
        Where are the longest delays expected?
        A   between junctions 10 and 11
        B   between junctions 13 and 14
        C   between junctions 17 and 18

8   You hear a man phoning his local newsagent's shop.
        Which newspaper did he receive by mistake this morning?
        A   *the Telegraph*
        B   *the Sun*
        C   *the Daily Mirror*

Part 1
Part 2
Part 3
Part 4

Track 14

You will hear a golfer called John Freeman giving a talk about his career. For questions **9–18**, complete the sentences with a word or short phrase.

Golf

John Freeman has been playing golf for (**9**) .... years.

John's father never progressed as a golfer because he couldn't afford very good (**10**) ....

When he was younger, John wanted to be a professional (**11**) .... player.

John's father took up golf again after being (**12**) ....

John wishes he had received some (**13**) .... from his teachers at school,

John says that golf is often seen as a sport for people with a lot of (**14**) ....

Young golfers should be able to get help from (**15**) ....

The (**16**) .... of British players is likely to raise the profile of golf.

John's income from golf is (**17**) ....

John used to dye his hair (**18**) ....

PAPER 1 Reading and
          Use of English
PAPER 2 Writing
PAPER 3 Listening
PAPER 4 Speaking

Part 1
Part 2
Part 3
Part 4

Track 15

You will hear five short extracts in which people are talking about holidays. For questions **19–23**, choose from the list (**A–H**) what each speaker says. Use the letters only once. There are three extra letters which you do not need to use.

A   It made our friendship stronger.

B   I realised I loved long journeys.

Speaker 1   19

C   It gave me a sense of my origins.

Speaker 2   20

D   It provided an escape.

Speaker 3   21

E   I felt closer to my family.

Speaker 4   22

F   It was my first holiday abroad.

Speaker 5   23

G   I felt I had learnt something.

H   I was relieved to be back home.

PAPER 1 Reading and
Use of English

PAPER 2 Writing

PAPER 3 Listening

PAPER 4 Speaking

Part 1
Part 2
Part 3
Part 4

Track 16

You will hear part of a radio interview with Laura Bartlett, who works as a florist (someone who sells and arranges flowers). For questions **24–30**, choose the best answer (**A**, **B** or **C**).

24 Laura's parents
    A   were professional gardeners.
    B   had a successful florist's shop.
    C   loved cultivating plants.

25 Laura originally wanted
    A   to work as a graphic designer.
    B   to become an artist.
    C   to write articles for a magazine.

26 She became a florist
    A   because she didn't know what else to do.
    B   as soon as she resigned from the magazine.
    C   as the result of an accident.

27 In the beginning, Laura
    A   wasn't skilled at working with flowers.
    B   didn't work with flowers at all.
    C   only delivered flowers to customers.

28 Laura had to learn
    A   the names of different species of flowers.
    B   which flowers florists could use in their work.
    C   how to prepare flowers for arrangements.

29 Laura suggests that a young person who wants to be a florist must be prepared
    A   to send flowers to people who are ill.
    B   to work long hours at certain times of the year.
    C   to spend a lot of time at the flower market.

30 Laura advises young people who would like to become florists
    A   to work at a florist's while they are attending courses in floristry.
    B   to study floristry full time at a college before they get a job.
    C   to learn how to program a computer.

PAPER 1   Reading and
             Use of English

PAPER 2   Writing

PAPER 3   Listening

PAPER 4   Speaking

Part 1 (2 minutes)

The examiner (interlocutor) will ask each of you to speak briefly in turn and to give personal information about yourselves. You can expect a variety of questions, such as:

How did you travel here today?
What sort of public transport is available in this area?
What form of transport do you use most often? (Why?)
What do you like and dislike about it?

Part 2 (4 minutes)

You will each be asked to talk for a minute without interruption. You will each be given two different photographs in turn to talk about. After your partner has finished speaking, you will be asked a brief question connected with your partner's photographs.

1 At work

Look at the two photographs on page 168 which show people working in different environments

Candidate A, compare these photographs, and say how you think the people are feeling in these different situations.

Candidate B, which of these jobs would you prefer to do? (Why?)

2 Leisure

Look at the two photographs on page 169 which show people doing different leisure activities.

Candidate B, compare these photographs, and say what sort of person you think would enjoy each of these activities.

Candidate A, which of these activities would you prefer to do? (Why?)

Part 3 (4 minutes)

You will be asked to discuss something together without interruption by the examiner. You will have a page of ideas with a question to help you.

Inventions

Imagine that you are taking part in a television programme about inventions that have changed the course of history. Turn to page 170 which has the names of different inventions and a question for you to discuss. Talk to each other about how these different inventions have changed people's lives. Then decide which two have been the most important.

Part 4 (4 minutes)

The examiner will encourage you to develop the topic of your discussion in Part 3 by asking questions such as:

What are the advantages and disadvantages of using computers?
Do you think technological advances help to improve everyday life? (Why? / Why not?)
What are the disadvantages of modern technology?
Do you think we rely too much on modern technology? (Why? / Why not?)
What inventions could improve people's lives in the future?
How do you think technology will be different in the future?

PAPER 1 Reading and Use of English

▶▶ PART 5

zip (v) to move quickly

thrust (v) to push hard

spring (v) to jump

run late (v) to be later than planned

foam (n) soft sponge-like material

undo (v) to defeat

retreat (n) a quiet place away from crowds

mixing board (n) electronic device for combining audio signals

embedded (adj) permanently part of

cheesy (adj) in bad style

bubble (n) a place where the outside world cannot disturb

constitute (v) to be or form

pitch (v) to put up

fundamental (adj) important, main

din (n) loud continuous noise

cocoon (n) protected place

thrill (n) great excitement

shove (v) to push hard

clamour (n) noise made by a lot of people

counteract (v) to reduce the effect of

babble (n) noise made by many people talking at once

traffic-choked (adj) completely full of traffic

retreat (v) to escape from

savour (v) to enjoy

bliss (n) great pleasure

sonic (adj) of sound

▶▶ PART 6

sphere (n) a ball shape

drift (v) to move slowly in water, pulled by the sea current

adjustment (n) small change

submersible (adj) designed to go underwater

crammed (adj) pushed together in a small space

maze (n) an area in which you can easily get lost because there are lots of similar paths

abundance (n) large number

drag (v) to pull

school of fish (n) large number of fish of the same species swimming together

disrupt (v) to disturb

re-establish (v) to exist in large numbers again

dim (adj) not bright

glide (v) to move elegantly and smoothly

soar (v) to rise quickly

countless (adj) a very large number

dazzling (adj) very bright

wreck (n) remains of a ship that has sunk

hover (v) to stay above a surface in one place

vent (n) a small opening

façade (n) the front of a building

▶▶ PART 7

gear (n) one of several speeds in a vehicle

tremble (v) to shake with fear

instructor (n) a teacher

ambition (n) a desire to succeed, a goal, an objective

attempt (n) an effort

regulation (n) a rule

save up (phr v) to collect money for a particular purpose

decent (adj) proper, good enough

put off (phr v) to make you dislike something or not want to do something

For questions **1–8**, read the text below and decide which word (**A, B, C** or **D**) best fits each gap. There is an example at the beginning (**0**).

Mark your answers **on the separate answer sheet**.

Example:

| 0 | **A** doubt | **B** reason | **C** purpose | **D** motive |

| 0 | **A** | **B** | **C** | **D** |

A powerful influence

There can be no (**0**) .... at all that the internet has made a huge difference to our lives. However, there is some concern over whether people spend too much time browsing the internet or playing computer games, (**1**) .... ever doing anything else in their spare time. Are these activities genuinely (**2**) .... to our well-being? Does spending too much time chatting on social networking sites really (**3**) .... our ability to form meaningful relationships in real life?

Quite the reverse, (**4**) .... to some social media experts, who suggest that using websites to keep in touch with friends may (**5**) .... help to enhance personal relationships and provide people with an increased (**6**) .... of belonging.

There may be room for argument in (**7**) .... of limiting time spent online, especially when it may break into study or work time. Research, however, also indicates that spending a healthy amount of time in front of a computer doesn't necessarily (**8**) .... with academic performance.

1	**A** nearly	**B** literally	**C** almost	**D** hardly
2	**A** harming	**B** harmful	**C** hurting	**D** hurtful
3	**A** affect	**B** bother	**C** effect	**D** concern
4	**A** agreeing	**B** corresponding	**C** owing	**D** according
5	**A** completely	**B** probably	**C** actually	**D** rightly
6	**A** function	**B** sense	**C** attitude	**D** meaning
7	**A** favour	**B** help	**C** choice	**D** opinion
8	**A** trouble	**B** interrupt	**C** oppose	**D** interfere

PAPER 1 Reading and ▸   Part 1
        Use of English   Part 2

PAPER 2 Writing   Part 3
                            Part 4
PAPER 3 Listening   Part 5

PAPER 4 Speaking   Part 6
                            Part 7

For questions **9–16**, read the text below and think of the word which best fits each gap. Use only **one** word in each gap. There is an example at the beginning (**0**).

Write your answers **IN CAPITAL LETTERS on the separate answer sheet**.

Example: | 0 | W | H | O |

Driving blind

The idea that a blind person could drive a car sounds crazy. And the concept of someone (**0**) .... can't see driving a car at almost 150 miles per hour sounds even crazier. Miranda Naylor, (**9**) .... blind accountant from the UK, has done exactly that in an attempt (**10**) .... raise money for charity. Mrs Naylor drove a sports car for two miles along the runway of a disused airfield. She was (**11**) .... radio contact with her husband, who gave her directions and advice. Her achievement (**12**) .... expected to raise about £50,000, which will be donated to a company that trains dogs for (**13**) .... blind.

Mrs Naylor (**14**) .... been blind since she was six, and still has some visual memories of the world around her. She admits that (**15**) .... having sight makes life awkward (**16**) .... times, but she says, 'Achieving something can be a great source of self-confidence.' Miranda is now looking for a new challenge and wants to try motorbiking.

PAPER 1	Reading and Use of English	▶
PAPER 2	Writing	
PAPER 3	Listening	
PAPER 4	Speaking	

Part 1
Part 2
Part 3
Part 4
Part 5
Part 6
Part 7

For questions **17–24**, read the text below. Use the word given in capitals at the end of some of the lines to form a word that fits in the gap **in the same line**. There is an example at the beginning (**0**).

Write your answers **IN CAPITAL LETTERS on the separate answer sheet**.

Example: `0` `E` `X` `C` `I` `T` `I` `N` `G` `` `` `` `` `` `` `` `` ``

Following swallows

Bert Cook's job doesn't immediately strike you as (**0**) ....   **EXCITE**
He sits inside a small construction made of cloth and wire and
watches birds: swallows, in fact, whose (**17**) .... in Britain after   **ARRIVE**
a dangerous flight marks the (**18**) .... of summer. The severe   **BEGIN**
weather caused by (**19**) .... warming makes their journey   **GLOBE**
tougher each year.

One of their main (**20**) .... is getting enough to eat. Insect   **DIFFICULT**
numbers have declined (**21**) .... , and if the birds do make   **SHARP**
it to Britain, they may still die of (**22**) ....   **HUNGRY**

Farm buildings such as barns have been converted into
houses, and as a result, there are now fewer places for birds
to nest. Bert finds it (**23**) .... to say with any precision how   **POSSIBLE**
far the numbers of swallows have declined in the area
under (**24**) .... Bird populations can increase considerably   **OBSERVE**
if swallows have had a good breeding season, and for the
moment at least, scientists are not overly worried.

PAPER 1 Reading and Use of English ▶

PAPER 2 Writing

PAPER 3 Listening

PAPER 4 Speaking

Part 1
Part 2
Part 3
Part 4
Part 5
Part 6
Part 7

For questions **25–30**, complete the second sentence so that it has a similar meaning to the first sentence, using the word given. **Do not change the word given**. You must use between **two** and **five** words, including the word given. Here is an example (**0**).

Example:

0   I'll be very happy when I go on holiday.

    FORWARD

    I'm .... on holiday.

The gap can be filled by the words 'looking forward to going' so you write:

Example: | 0 | LOOKING FORWARD TO GOING |

Write **only** the missing words **IN CAPITAL LETTERS on the separate answer sheet**.

---

25   Our teacher always makes us do our homework before we leave the class.

    ALLOWS

    Our teacher .... leave the class until we've done our homework.

26   It was almost dark when we got home.

    UNTIL

    We .... it was almost dark.

27   Peter woke up early because he didn't want to miss his flight.

    THAT

    Peter woke up early .... not miss his flight.

28   'You'd better not go for a walk,' said my father.

    ADVISED

    My father .... for a walk.

29   I wish I hadn't left the window open.

    SHOULD

    I .... the window open.

30   All the guests enjoyed themselves at the party apart from George.

    WHO

    George was the .... enjoy himself at the party.

PAPER 1	Reading and ▶	Part 1
	Use of English	Part 2
PAPER 2	Writing	Part 3
		Part 4
PAPER 3	Listening	**Part 5**
PAPER 4	Speaking	Part 6
		Part 7

You are going to read an article about photography. For questions **31–36**, choose the answer (**A**, **B**, **C** or **D**) which you think fits best according to the text.

Mark your answers **on the separate answer sheet**.

Photo research

Photographer Jim Richardson tells us how he aims to get the most from photo shoots.

'If you want to be a better photographer, stand in front of better stuff.' That's a simple mantra and I repeat it over and over to myself. I share it with other photographers and I endeavour to follow my own advice. As a result, I spend a great deal of time doing photo research, looking for great locations to shoot. Put simply, I'm a better photographer when I'm standing in front of something wonderful like the Grand Canyon in Arizona, USA.

Seeing wonderful places is bread-and-butter photography – it's just part of the job. But getting there is only half of any great photograph's story. The other half is how the photographer prepares to capture the subject once in front of it. Example: today my mind is absorbed in the long climb up Skellig Michael, a remote island isolated in the Atlantic Ocean off the coast of Ireland, where Celtic monks found their solace in spiritual isolation 1,400 years ago. I have never been on Skellig Michael, though I have come close four times. Each time I was held back by high seas. In my head I am getting ready to be among the little huts in the monastery at the summit, in the mindset of those who sought their spirituality in the vast Atlantic all those years ago.

In four days I'll be setting sail on a cruise of the British and Irish Isles, and I'll have a chance once again to ascend the slopes of Skellig Michael. I want to be ready to seize the day. For me, groundwork is part of photography, as essential as knowing exposure and lighting or recognising the decisive moment to take the shot. Research sounds like a boring task to many photographers, but for others, digging into a subject in advance is part of the pleasure. I'm one of those photographers.

Philosophically, photographers seem to divide along that line. On one side are those who desire only to be in the moment. On the other side are the planners. These folks would never dream of going out the door without a full list of how they're going to approach the shoot. (Actually, there is a third group nowadays. They just capture the whole scene and do all the creative work in Photoshop after the event.) Fortunately, it doesn't have to be an either/or decision. Most photographers I know do both: research extensively to prepare their schedule (and their minds) and then act in the moment once on site.

I do extensive research in order to get ready for a photographic trip. This includes creating a file for each location I'm due to visit. For my upcoming cruise I already know where we are going day by day. So I start a file for each place and begin to compile information. Knowing what the place looks like in advance is invaluable, so I'll hit several internet photo sites. Besides clueing me in to the photographic possibilities of the location, this can also show me what angles have already become overused and which I should line 29 therefore avoid. But I'll also find angles I didn't expect from locations I hadn't imagined. Armed with these I'll be better prepared to push the boundaries of what people expect.

Above all, I'll look for places and events that are seasonal and timeless. I open my mind to what might make a great subject for a picture. Most travellers tend to think only of places they're visiting, without looking deeper into culture, history or meaning. I try to get in time with the rhythm of the place and in tune with its melody. But most of all I just want to be ready. If I'm ready, I can just about count on being lucky.

31 What is Jim trying to do in the first paragraph?

    A convince the reader that his method of working is appropriate
    B explain his approach towards taking good photographs
    C remind himself that he should listen to the ideas of others
    D clarify what makes a location good to photograph

32 Why does Jim provide an example in the second paragraph?

    A to explain why he hasn't managed to visit Skellig Michael before
    B to describe what he imagines the next place he will visit to be like
    C to offer details of what he has discovered about Skellig Michael
    D to show how he prepares herself mentally before going to a new place

33 How does Jim feel about the cruise he will go on?

    A excited about an opportunity he didn't think he would get
    B uncertain whether he will know when to take the best photo
    C confident he will produce better work than other photographers
    D uninterested in certain aspects of preparing for travel

34 What point does Jim make about photographers in the fourth paragraph?

    A They are unable to decide on the best plan of action.
    B It is possible for them to adopt flexible ways of working.
    C Some of them refuse to try to understand the way others work.
    D The third group are not as imaginative as some of the others.

35 What does 'this' refer to in line 29?

    A having a daily plan of travel
    B knowing which angles to avoid
    C looking at photo websites
    D compiling location files

36 What does Jim suggest in the final paragraph?

    A He is careful about choosing the right place to visit.
    B Many people who travel don't understand what they see.
    C He likes to go to places that few people bother to visit.
    D Some travellers don't spend enough time in a place.

PAPER 1	Reading and	▶	Part 1
	Use of English		Part 2
PAPER 2	Writing		Part 3
			Part 4
PAPER 3	Listening		Part 5
PAPER 4	Speaking		**Part 6**
			Part 7

You are going to read a newspaper article about orangutans. Six sentences have been removed from the article. Choose from the sentences **A–G** the one which fits each gap (**37–42**). There is one extra sentence which you do not need to use.

Mark your answers **on the separate answer sheet**.

Almost human

Orangutans and chimpanzees are capable of performing intellectual feats we once thought to be uniquely human. Using language, being self-aware, learning by imitation and problem-solving are high-level abilities that are not limited to humans. Research has shown that orangutans and other great apes, like chimpanzees and gorillas, share these abilities too.

There are several projects studying the use of language by these creatures. Understanding their mechanisms of developing language will help us evaluate our own linguistic abilities. One of the orangutans involved in a project in Virginia, USA, has learnt how to use over 100 words in sign language, the language used by the deaf to communicate with each other. Another orangutan, Hannah, has learnt 13 symbols that represent different nouns and verbs. Hannah can combine the symbols into simple commands like 'open bag'. **37**

Not really. One of the fundamental elements of human thought is the ability to recognise numbers and express ideas with them within meaningful strings of words. Hannah can recognise numbers from one to three with reasonable accuracy. **38**

A fundamental difference between humans and orangutans is their ability to comprehend abstract ideas. Abstract concepts are basic to human thinking, while there's little evidence that orangutans can understand abstract ideas at all.

One of the most interesting experiments in the Virginia project concerns memory. **39** Orangutans, on the other hand, appear to do so according to where they saw them last. This seems a less efficient way of storing information, so it may well be that orangutans have a limited capacity for memory in comparison to humans.

40 They feel extremely frustrated when they make an error and they never rush into a task because they don't want to be wrong. Orangutans have idiosyncracies and differences in character. Some are slow learners, while others are more impulsive.

Unfortunately, most of the research on great ape intelligence has been done with animals in captivity. **41** Studies of orangutans, however, that suffered captivity but were then freed showed that they are capable of learning by imitation. Imitating someone yawn or scratch his head is not a great intellectual accomplishment, but learning a new behaviour just by watching is a very advanced ability. Orangutans could chop firewood or wash dishes without being taught. The only way they could have done it was by watching humans.

Compared to orangutans, chimpanzees are genetically closer to human beings and they are thought to be more intelligent. There are differences in the way the minds of chimps and orangutans work. **42** The chimps seem to work fast, almost intuitively, while orangutans are slower and more methodical.

One feature of both chimps and orangutans is the ability to recognise themselves in a mirror. This seems to suggest that they both have a concept of 'self' – they know who they are and think of themselves in a particular way. Chimpanzees are manipulative and capable of deception. They are very good problem-solvers, clearly capable of complex cognitive performance, which makes them almost human.

A Orangutans can become very emotional when they fail a test.

B One obvious disadvantage is that we cannot study their behaviour in their natural environment.

C Does this mean she is starting to think in a human way?

D None of these tasks can be performed well by orangutans.

E Humans generally remember things by putting them into groups or categories.

F However, she hasn't yet learnt to use them in sentences.

G This becomes apparent when they are each given the same task to do.

PAPER 1	Reading and Use of English	▶	Part 1
PAPER 2	Writing		Part 2
PAPER 3	Listening		Part 3
PAPER 4	Speaking		Part 4
			Part 5
			Part 6
			Part 7

You are going to read a magazine article in which four people talk about running the London Marathon. For questions **43–52** choose from the people (**A–D**). The people may be chosen more than once.

Mark your answers **on the separate answer sheet**.

Which person

didn't like the reactions of the watching crowd?	**43**
began running to accompany a runner?	**44**
didn't finish last year's marathon?	**45**
had an unpleasant experience in his or her first marathon?	**46**
entered the marathon with colleagues from work?	**47**
is not confident about his or her physical condition?	**48**
belongs to a sports group?	**49**
trains under bad weather conditions?	**50**
saw himself or herself on television?	**51**
doesn't have to go far for his or her runs?	**52**

Running for fun

A Peter Chamberlain

I was always keen on sports. Running a long distance is a bit like life too. You start with a sense of anticipation, you go through some great highs and terrible lows, but in the end it seems to be worth it. There is nothing that I enjoy more than a good workout at the gym or a good one-hour run across the local wildlife reserve. Fortunately, where I live, I can reach the open countryside in just a couple of minutes on foot from my front-door step. In my case, participation in the London Marathon was not about winning, it was about doing the best you possibly can. My first marathon was a disaster. Everything was going fine until the twelfth mile when I started to feel a bit of fatigue kicking in and hit the wall between the fourteenth and fifteenth miles.

B Rosalind Masterson

I surprised myself by doing so well, to tell you the truth. It all started when a friend of mine was training for the marathon and asked me to join her a few mornings a week. I didn't think I was very fit when I started, although years ago I'd go cycling three times a week and jogging at weekends. I found the experience enjoyable but realised I preferred jogging on my own. Success depends a lot on your mood. Last year, for example, I was feeling very stressed for one reason or another, and I got tired much more quickly; I didn't even get to the end of the course! This year's been completely different. London was such a success that I've entered for the Berlin Marathon next month, along with three friends. My husband thinks I'm mad, though when we watched the news that night and he could see my face among the crowds, he was fairly impressed.

C Ruth Watson

Long-distance running is not about how fast you can run, it's about how much pain you can take. Long-distance running is a good discipline for life itself. I run with my head and my heart, because physically I don't think I've got a great deal of talent or ability. I was always a very energetic sports person and I have entered the marathon five times so far. Last year I managed to complete a half marathon in 90 minutes, which was quite an accomplishment for someone who did not train systematically. One thing that annoyed me in my last marathon was the attitude of people watching. They took more interest in the fun-runners and celebrities than in the battle of the elite runners chasing qualification times for the Olympic Games.

D John Saddler

An old friend of mine has been a member of a jogging club for years, and he finally persuaded me to go along with him one Saturday to see if I would enjoy it. Well, I felt fairly good afterwards, so I joined the club and started thinking seriously about running. I thought that entering for the marathon would give me a unique opportunity to raise some cash for the Red Cross. In fact, four of us from the office decided to do the same thing, and between us we raised over £25,000, which was great! Running wasn't as hard as I expected. Training can be difficult, especially when it means I have to drag myself out of bed on cold winter mornings and go jogging in the pouring rain. I never train with friends because I find it impossible to concentrate on what I'm doing.

PAPER 1 Reading and
            Use of English
PAPER 2 Writing ▶ | Part 1 | Part 2 |
PAPER 3 Listening
PAPER 4 Speaking

You **must** answer this question. Write your answer in **140–190** words in an appropriate style.

1 You have been discussing families in your English class. Now, your teacher has asked you to write an essay for homework.

Write an essay using **all** the notes and give reasons for your point of view.

> Growing up in a large family is better than being brought up in a small one. Do you agree?
>
> **Notes**
> Write about:
>
> 1. attention from parents
> 2. relationships with brothers and sisters
> 3. .... (your own idea)

PAPER 1 Reading and
Use of English

PAPER 2 Writing ▶ Part 1

PAPER 3 Listening   Part 2

PAPER 4 Speaking

Write an answer to one of the questions **2–5** in this part. Write your answer in **140–190** words in an appropriate style.

2   You see this announcement in an English-language music magazine.

> **Do you enjoy listening to traditional music?**
>
> Do you think traditional music from your country is old-fashioned, or should it continue to be promoted in the modern world? If so, how is it possible to get more people interested in traditional music?
>
> We'd love to receive your articles. The best one will be published next month!

Write your **article**.

3   This is part of an email you have received from your English-speaking friend, Kim.

> I heard you've moved from the city to a small country village. Can you tell me about it? What are the differences between living in each of the places? How do you feel about the change in lifestyle?
>
> I can't wait to hear from you!
>
> Kim

Write your **email**.

4   You recently saw this notice in an English-language magazine called *TV News*:

> Send us your review of the best or worst TV programme you have seen this year. Include information on what the programme was about and say what made the programme so good/bad. Do you think another programme should be made on the same theme?
>
> We will publish the best reviews in a special summer supplement.

Write your **review**.

5   (*for FIRST FOR SCHOOLS candidates only*)

Answer the following question based on your reading of **one** of the set books.

Your friend has asked you to recommend something to read on holiday. Write a **letter** to your friend about the book you have read, giving reasons why this particular book would be suitable for him/her.

PAPER 1 Reading and
Use of English

PAPER 2 Writing

PAPER 3 Listening   ▶
Part 1
Part 2
Part 3
Part 4

PAPER 4 Speaking

Track 17

You will hear people talking in eight different situations. For questions **1–8**, choose the best answer (**A**, **B** or **C**).

1 You hear a tour guide talking about her job.
   What does she like best about being a tour guide?
   A the places she visits
   B the people she works with
   C the different types of food she eats

2 You hear the start of a radio programme about cars.
   Who is the guest on this programme?
   A a car designer
   B an electrical engineer
   C a mechanic

3 You hear a businesswoman talking to her assistant.
   What does she want him to do?
   A write a report
   B make a phone call
   C send an email

4 You hear two friends talking about an evening out.
   Where did they go?
   A to the cinema
   B to the theatre
   C to a party

5 You hear a man talking about his aunt.
   What was her profession?
   A doctor
   B lawyer
   C actress

6 You hear a brother and sister talking about a present for their mother.
   What have they bought?
   A a book
   B a DVD
   C a cooking pot

7 You hear an announcement in a multiplex cinema.
   Which screen is showing the film *Racing Fever*?
   A screen 3
   B screen 5
   C screen 6

8 You hear a ballet dancer talking about an injury.
   What part of his body has he hurt?
   A his back
   B his feet
   C his arm

PAPER 1 Reading and
          Use of English

PAPER 2 Writing

PAPER 3 Listening ▶

PAPER 4 Speaking

Part 1
Part 2
Part 3
Part 4

🎧 **Track 18**

You will hear part of a talk by a man called David Barns, who is the director of a company that will be building a new shopping mall. For questions **9–18**, complete the sentences with a word or short phrase.

Whitesea shopping mall

The mall is expected to open in (**9**) .... next year.

The total cost will be (**10**) .... billion pounds.

A new (**11**) .... will be built next to the shopping mall.

The car park will be situated (**12**) .... and will have spaces for 3,000 cars.

Three (**13**) .... will be provided to help shoppers with children.

One section of the mall has a (**14**) ....

There will be (**15**) .... cinemas showing a wide range of the current films.

(**16**) .... films will be shown twice a day.

There will be walkways with (**17**) .... between different areas of the mall.

There will be an exhibition focusing on the (**18**) .... of the area.

PAPER 1 Reading and
           Use of English
PAPER 2 Writing
PAPER 3 Listening ▶
           Part 1
           Part 2
           Part 3
           Part 4
PAPER 4 Speaking

🎧 **Track 19**

You will hear five short extracts in which people are talking about how they got their current jobs. For questions **19–23**, choose from the list (**A–H**) what each speaker says. Use the letters only once. There are three extra letters which you do not need to use.

A I'd done some unpaid work experience at the company.

B I saw an advertisement on a careers website.

Speaker 1 [   ] 19

C I had a contact who worked at the company.

Speaker 2 [   ] 20

D I heard about it from a friend.

Speaker 3 [   ] 21

E I was lucky with a phone call.

Speaker 4 [   ] 22

F I approached the boss face to face.

Speaker 5 [   ] 23

G I was promoted from a previous position.

H I found out about the company through social media.

🎧 **Track 20**

You will hear a radio interview with a doctor called Ann Winters, who is an expert on memory. For questions **24–30**, choose the best answer (**A**, **B** or **C**).

24 Ann compares the human memory to a hard drive because
    A both can be negatively affected by external factors.
    B both can be trained to expand and improve.
    C both can store an unlimited number of images.

25 We are told that people suffering from Alzheimer's disease
    A don't understand the mechanism of life.
    B can't remember who they are.
    C forget how to perform simple tasks.

26 Research has shown that people who have mentally active jobs
    A will never develop Alzheimer's disease.
    B are more likely to develop Alzheimer's disease.
    C are less likely to develop Alzheimer's disease.

27 Apparently, our memories are harmed by
    A doing too many physical exercises.
    B devices designed to help us remember things.
    C forcing ourselves to try to remember too much.

28 Ann says we can remember things if we
    A connect them with a physical object.
    B look at them very carefully first.
    C encourage people to remind us about them.

29 The technique Ann describes works best for people
    A who like pictures.
    B who are used to abstract thought.
    C who can visualise ideas well.

30 Doing crosswords is an example of activities that
    A can prevent ageing.
    B can extend life expectancy.
    C can delay memory decline.

PAPER 1 Reading and
         Use of English

PAPER 2 Writing

PAPER 3 Listening

PAPER 4 Speaking

Part 1 (2 minutes)

The examiner (interlocutor) will ask each of you to speak briefly in turn and to give personal information about yourselves. You can expect a variety of questions, such as:

Who do you prefer to spend your free time with? (Why?)
Do you prefer to spend your free time outdoors or indoors? (Why?)
What kinds of things do you like doing with your friends / family?
What's your favourite part of the day? (Why?)

Part 2 (4 minutes)

You will each be asked to talk for a minute without interruption. You will each be given two different photographs in turn to talk about. After your partner has finished speaking, you will be asked a brief question connected with your partner's photographs.

1 Means of transport

Look at the two photographs on page 171 which show different forms of transport.

Candidate A, compare these photographs, and say why you think people use these different means of transport.

Candidate B, which of these means of transport do you prefer to use? (Why?)

2 Fashion

Look at the two photographs on page 172 which show different sorts of clothes.

Candidate B, compare these photographs, and say why you think the people have chosen to wear these sorts of clothes.

Candidate A, which of these sorts of clothes do you prefer to wear? (Why?)

Part 3 (4 minutes)

You will be asked to discuss something together without interruption by the examiner. You will have a page of ideas and a question to help you.

Environmental problems

Imagine you are helping to prepare a poster to raise environmental awareness in your area. Turn to page 173 which has ideas for images that could be included and a question for you to discuss. Talk to each other about which images on a poster would be useful to raise environmental awareness. Then decide which two images should be included.

Part 4 (4 minutes)

The examiner will encourage you to develop the topic of your discussion in Part 3 by asking questions such as:

Are school clubs and societies, such as a photographic club and a computer club, useful for students? (Why? / Why not?)

What kind of after-school activity did you or would you enjoy at school? (Why?)

What do you think people learn from activities which are not connected with schoolwork?

Should schools try to become active parts of the local community? (Why? / Why not?)

How can schools raise people's environmental awareness?

What other useful things can schools teach young people?

PAPER 1 Reading and Use of English

▶▶ PART 5

mantra (n) a commonly repeated word or phrase

endeavour (v) to try very hard to do something

capture (v) to record something by camera/on film

be absorbed in (adj) to give all your attention to something that you are doing

remote (adj) far away

solace (n) comfort

summit (n) the highest point of a mountain

mindset (n) mental attitude

ascend (v) to go up

seize the day (phr) to enjoy the moment

groundwork (n) preparation

exposure (n) the length of time light falls on the digital sensor/film (photography)

decisive moment (n) perfect, ideal time

dig into (v) to find out about

approach (v) to deal with

compile (v) to put together

invaluable (adj) extremely useful

clue in (v) to provide someone with a clue

angle (n) the direction from which you look at something

push the boundaries (expr) to experiment

timeless (adj) unaffected by time

be in tune with (expr) understand

▶▶ PART 6

intellectual (adj) related to thinking

evaluate (v) to estimate worth, to determine the value of something

accuracy (n) something that is correct and true

fundamental (adj) basic, primary

comprehend (v) to get the meaning of something, to understand

capacity (n) the ability to do something

idiosyncrasy (n) an odd habit or characteristic

impulsive (adj) doing things without considering the possible dangers or problems

captivity (n) a condition of holding someone or something by force against their will, confinement, imprisonment

accomplishment (n) a difficult task done well, success, achievement

genetically (adv) related to genes or genetics

intuitively (adv) related to feelings, not learnt knowledge, instinctive

methodical (adj) systematic, careful, in a step-by-step manner

apparent (adj) obvious, clear

▶▶ PART 7

anticipation (n) pleasant expectation

workout (n) a session of physical exercise

fatigue (n) great tiredness

kick in (phr v) to begin to have an effect

hit the wall (phr) to collapse, to be unable to go on

enter for (phr v) to put your name on the list of people taking part in something

impress (v) to cause others to admire

discipline (n) training

persuade (v) to lead a person or group to believe or do something by arguing or reasoning with them

pouring (adj) raining hard

For questions **1–8**, read the text below and decide which word (**A, B, C** or **D**) best fits each gap. There is an example at the beginning (**0**).

Mark your answers **on the separate answer sheet**.

Example:

0 **A** life   **B** living   **C** alive   **D** live

0	A	B	C	D

Old and active

It is a well-known fact that Japanese people have a longer (**0**) .... expectancy than the population of most other countries. They also expect to remain healthier for longer.

Scientists are trying to work (**1**) .... what keeps elderly Japanese people so healthy, and whether there is a lesson to be (**2**) .... from their lifestyles. Should we (**3**) .... any changes to our eating habits, for instance? Is there some secret (**4**) .... in the Japanese diet that is particularly (**5**) .... for the human body?

Although the (**6**) .... of a longer, healthier life is a good thing for the individual, it can (**7**) .... create a social problem. The number of people over the age of 65 in the population has doubled in the last 50 years. Japan could soon be (**8**) .... an economic problem: there are more elderly people who need to be looked after, and relatively fewer younger people working and paying taxes to support them.

1 **A** for	**B** out	**C** in	**D** off
2 **A** learnt	**B** gathered	**C** understood	**D** gained
3 **A** do	**B** make	**C** set	**D** give
4 **A** ingredient	**B** component	**C** portion	**D** helping
5 **A** caring	**B** supportive	**C** positive	**D** beneficial
6 **A** view	**B** outlook	**C** prospect	**D** wish
7 **A** therefore	**B** actually	**C** even	**D** as well
8 **A** facing	**B** meeting	**C** adopting	**D** obtaining

For questions **9–16,** read the text below and think of the word which best fits each gap. Use only **one** word in each gap. There is an example at the beginning (**0**).

Write your answers **IN CAPITAL LETTERS on the separate answer sheet**.

Example: | 0 | B Y | | | | | | | | | | | | | | | | | | | |

Acoustic archaeology

Acoustic archaeology studies the role played (**0**) .... sound in the ancient world. It examines the connection (**9**) .... acoustics and religious or spiritual sites. The main question is whether the acoustics of a place are relevant to the way (**10**) .... was used.

Archaeologists have noticed that a number of ancient sites have echoes at very low frequencies. When sounds are as low as this, you feel them in your body, rather (**11**) .... just hearing them, and this creates a feeling of happiness and contentment.

If you stand in (**12**) .... of the Maya Temple in Mexico and clap your hands, you can hear an echo that sounds (**13**) .... the chirp of the Maya sacred bird. This echo (**14**) .... produced because the steps of the long temple staircase are at different distances from the listener. Some archaeologists claim that the Maya deliberately constructed this temple (**15**) .... achieve this sound. Similar acoustic phenomena have been observed in sites (**16**) .... over the world.

PAPER 1	Reading and ▸	Part 1
	Use of English	Part 2
PAPER 2	Writing	**Part 3**
		Part 4
PAPER 3	Listening	Part 5
PAPER 4	Speaking	Part 6
		Part 7

For questions **17–24,** read the text below. Use the word given in capitals at the end of some of the lines to form a word that fits in the gap **in the same line**. There is an example at the beginning (**0**).

Write your answers **IN CAPITAL LETTERS on the separate answer sheet.**

Example: | 0 | C | O | M | P | E | T | I | T | I | V | E | | | | | | | |

The sport of kings

The (**0**) .... racing of horses is one of humankind's most ancient sports. Horse racing was an organised sport in all major (**17**) .... from Central Asia to the Mediterranean and became an (**18**) .... with the public in the Roman Empire. The sport has (**19**) .... been associated with royalty and the nobility. It became a professional sport at the beginning of the eighteenth century. It is the second most (**20**) .... attended spectator sport in the US, after baseball.

COMPETE

CIVILISE

OBSESS

TRADITION

WIDE

In the UK, the Jockey Club, founded in 1750, has complete (**21**) .... for horse racing. It is also responsible for the (**22**) .... regarding the breeding of racehorses. Although science has been (**23**) .... to find a breeding system that guarantees the birth of a champion, it is possible to produce horses that are successful on the racetrack. Commercial breeding is a very (**24**) .... business, and racehorses can be worth millions of pounds.

RESPONSIBLE

REGULATE

ABLE

PROFIT

For questions **25–30**, complete the second sentence so that it has a similar meaning to the first sentence, using the word given. **Do not change the word given.** You must use between **two** and **five** words, including the word given. Here is an example (**0**).

Example:

0 I'll be very happy when I go on holiday.

FORWARD

I'm .... on holiday.

The gap can be filled by the words 'looking forward to going' so you write:

Example: | **0** | LOOKING FORWARD TO GOING |

Write **only** the missing words **IN CAPITAL LETTERS on the separate answer sheet.**

---

25 I don't know how wide that river is.

WHAT

I don't know .... of that river is.

26 Her parents didn't let her go to the rock concert.

ALLOWED

She .... go to the rock concert.

27 My father last went abroad in 2010.

BEEN

My father .... 2010.

28 'Did you read the book or not?' the teacher asked me.

WHETHER

The teacher asked me .... the book or not.

29 I find that kind of music really irritating.

GETS

That kind of music really .... nerves.

30 He cycled across Italy in three weeks.

HIM

It .... cycle across Italy.

You are going to read an article about a park in New York. For questions **31–36**, choose the answer (**A**, **B**, **C** or **D**) which you think fits best according to the text.

Mark your answers **on the separate answer sheet**.

Miracle above Manhattan

New Yorkers can relax over busy streets in an innovative park called the High Line.

Parks in large cities are usually thought of as refuges, as islands of green amid seas of concrete and steel. When you approach the High Line in the Chelsea neighbourhood on the lower west side of Manhattan, in New York, what you see first is the kind of thing urban parks were created to get away from – a harsh, heavy, black steel structure supporting an elevated rail line that once brought freight cars right into factories and warehouses and that looks, at least from a distance, more like some abandoned leftover from the past than an urban oasis.

line 7 Until recently that's precisely what the High Line was, and a crumbling one too. Many people couldn't wait to tear it down. Almost a decade later, it has been turned into one of the most innovative and inviting public spaces in New York City. The black steel columns that once supported abandoned train tracks now hold up an elevated park – part promenade, part town square, part botanical garden.

Walking on the High Line is unlike any other experience in New York. You float about eight metres above the ground, at once connected to street life and far away from it. You can sit surrounded by carefully tended plantings and take in the sun and the Hudson River views, or you can walk the line as it slices between old buildings and past striking new ones. I have walked the High Line dozens of times, and its vantage point, different from that of any street, sidewalk, or park, never ceases to surprise and delight. Not the least of the remarkable things about the High Line is the way, without streets to cross or traffic lights to wait for, ten blocks pass as quickly as two.

The High Line is a wonderful idea that was not only realised but turned out better than anyone had imagined. The real heroes of the story are Joshua David, a freelance writer who lived near the midsection of the High Line, and Robert Hammond, an artist who also lived nearby. 'I saw an article saying that the High Line was going to be demolished, and I wondered if anyone was going to try to save it,' Hammond said to me when I interviewed them. 'I was in love with the steel structure, the rivets, the ruin. I assumed that some civic group was going to try and preserve it, and I saw that it was on the agenda for a community meeting. I went to see what was going on, and Josh was sitting next to me. We were the only people at the meeting who were interested in saving it.'

'The railroad sent representatives who showed some plans to reuse it, which enraged the people who were trying to get it torn down,' David explained. 'That's what sparked the conversation between me and Robert – we couldn't believe the degree of rage some of those people had.' David and Hammond asked railroad officials to take them to look at the High Line. 'When we got up there, we saw a mile and a half of wildflowers in the middle of Manhattan. New Yorkers always dream of finding open space – it's a fantasy when you live in a studio apartment,' David said. And that's how the project began.

From the day the first section of the High Line park opened, it has been one of the city's major tourist attractions. Yet it is just as much a neighbourhood park. When I was there on a sunny day last autumn, a section the designers had designated as a kind of sundeck was jammed, and there seemed to be as many locals treating the area as the equivalent of their own beach as visitors out for a promenade. Sometimes dreams really do come true.

31 What does the writer say about the High Line park in the first paragraph?

    A It may initially appear unattractive.
    B It is most easily reached by train.
    C People may wonder where the plants are.
    D People are amazed to find out how old it is.

32 What does 'that' refer to in line 7?

    A an urban oasis
    B a black steel structure
    C a leftover from the past
    D a group of factories and warehouses

33 When walking on the High Line, the writer notices that

    A the weather seems much better there.
    B he seems to walk further in a shorter time.
    C new buildings keep being built around it.
    D he can see everything in the streets below.

34 Why did Robert Hammond go to the community meeting?

    A He was told about it by his friend Joshua David.
    B He was responding to an appeal for volunteers.
    C He believed other people there would share his views.
    D He thought he could persuade people to join his campaign.

35 How did Joshua David feel about what happened at the meeting?

    A pleased to realise they might succeed
    B encouraged by everyone's determination
    C worried that their way of life might change
    D surprised by the reaction to the ideas proposed

36 What does the writer say about the park in the final paragraph?

    A It satisfies a range of different needs.
    B Local people wish fewer tourists came to see it.
    C Some of its features are not being used as intended.
    D Its popularity has increased recently.

PAPER 1   Reading and ▶   Part 1
              Use of English   Part 2
PAPER 2   Writing   Part 3
                                    Part 4
PAPER 3   Listening   Part 5
PAPER 4   Speaking   Part 6
                                    Part 7

You are going to read a newspaper article about people who have difficulty counting. Six sentences have been removed from the article. Choose from the sentences **A–G** the one which fits each gap (**37–42**). There is one extra sentence, which you do not need to use.

Mark your answers **on the separate answer sheet**.

People who can't count

A recent study has discovered that dyscalculia, the mathematical equivalent of dyslexia, affects about 5% of children in Britain. An expert on the subject, Professor Maria Singelton, claims that the government should recognise dyscalculia, inform parents and teachers and provide support for those suffering from it. Unfortunately, there is no simple way of diagnosing dyscalculia and kids with this learning disability are usually labelled unintelligent.

37 Unlike most people, dyscalculics cannot recognise three or four objects unless they count them one by one. The majority of us, if shown three or four similar things, can immediately recognise them. People with dyscalculia have to go through the routine of counting even a small number of objects. For example, they need to count the three books on the table before they can say how many there are.

Dyscalculics have huge problems using numbers at all. They cannot understand, for instance, why two and three makes five. **38** Laboratory experiments have shown that animals such as monkeys and rats have developed a specific region of their brain to deal with numbers and related concepts. It's possible that dyscalculics, though intelligent, have not developed the part of the brain responsible for processing numbers.

Dyscalculics have difficulty with the abstract concept of time. **39** If your best friend is always late, he or she might be suffering from dyscalculia. Dyscalculics cannot keep track of time, they never know how much

time they have spent getting ready and how long it will take them to get to work.

You cannot rely on a dyscalculic to give you directions about how to get to the nearest train station. Inability to read maps and orientate themselves is common among dyscalculics. They may take a left turning instead of a right and end up miles away from their intended destination. **40**

Research has shown that they behave oddly in social situations like going shopping or having dinner at a restaurant. They never know how much they should tip the waiter or how much money they have got left after a shopping trip. **41** This poor ability in arithmetic can explain why they never know how much change they are due or what kind of budget they need for their summer holiday. Discalculia can also affect areas like sports or music. Dyscalculics cannot coordinate the movements of their body or remember the rules of games. They would find it impossible to recall the complicated step sequences of a dance and would rarely choose to do aerobics or play an instrument in their free time.

42 People suffering from discalculia can become painters, sculptors or poets. Dyscalculia does not seem to prevent or delay language acquisition. Dyscalculic children acquire language at the same time as, if not earlier than, most children and have no problem learning to read or write. Dyscalculia is a learning disability like dyslexia, not a general indication of intelligence.

A Another problem is not being able to tell, just by looking at two groups of objects, which group contains more objects than the other.

B On top of getting lost, they often misplace things and may spend endless hours looking for their car keys or passport.

C These stories are extremely upsetting for parents and children alike.

D What exactly is this learning disability in arithmetic?

E Dealing with cash, taking money from a cashpoint or using travellers' cheques can cause anxiety and fear.

F This can account for their difficulty in reading schedules and remembering the order in which things happened in the past.

G On the other hand, dyscalculics are very good at creative arts.

You are going to read an article in which four writers talk about the first book they wrote. For questions **43–52**, choose from the people (**A–D**). The writers may be chosen more than once.

Mark your answers **on the separate answer sheet.**

Which writer

took six months to write the book?	**43**
was upset at something their editor said?	**44**
did not like part of the book design?	**45**
had written the book years before it was published?	**46**
has never written that type of book since then?	**47**
produced a certain amount of writing each day?	**48**
revised the manuscript because the main character was boring?	**49**
wrote for a set amount of time each day?	**50**
wrote short stories before the first book?	**51**
won something for the first book?	**52**

The first book

A Harry Holden

I remember my first book very clearly; I suppose every writer does. But I also remember it because I've changed so much since then. It was a biography of the Duke of Wellington, which I'd been asked to write by a friend of mine, a publisher, who knew I was very interested in the subject. I'd had no experience of writing but I have to say the book was actually quite good. In fact, I was awarded the General Haig Memorial Prize for the book the year it was published. By the time it was finally finished, I was completely exhausted. I'd been working on it more or less full time for five years, and I vowed I'd never write a biography again. So since then, I've concentrated on detective stories. They're far easier!

B Marcia Onslow

My first book was quite successful, although to be completely frank, looking back, I think I was very lucky. I attended a creative writing course at university, intending to concentrate on short stories for magazines, which is quite a lucrative market. As a project in my final year, I was asked to write a long work of fiction, and I decided to write a love story set in America during the California gold rush. Anyway, I'd been advised to establish a strict schedule, so I would write ten pages every morning and correct them every evening. Then I left university, started writing stories for publication, and I more or less forgot about the book for about ten years, until my publisher suggested I might try writing a novel. So I just handed it to her, all finished, and she published it right away!

C Maria Delangelo

When I wrote the first draft of my first novel, *Chasing William,* it wasn't much like the version that was eventually published; my editor told me I would have to make some changes to the hero, William, because he wasn't interesting enough. Naturally, I was pretty offended at the time, but I'm glad to say I had the good sense to listen to my editor, who was completely right. The problem was that I had based the whole story on the real adventures of my uncle, William Hargreaves, simply describing my uncle's character. When you write a work of fiction, you have to make the main character intriguing, but describing a real person isn't always the best way to do that. Funnily enough, in the short stories I'd had published previously I never tried to use real people. I'm glad my editor talked me out of doing it in the novel.

D John Hopkins

I learnt a few important lessons from my first book, one of which is that you have to leave certain things to the publisher. For instance, the editor gave me a lot of advice about how to structure my book, a study of the Industrial Revolution. I was a bit hesitant in the beginning, but then I decided to follow his advice and I haven't regretted it. It was the same with the artistic work on the cover, which I really hated at first. But in the end the book was very successful, and I suppose the design must have been right. The other lesson I learnt   was about working methods. I'm quite an impetuous person, and I don't like being tied down to fixed ways of doing things. I discovered I had to be strict about how long I would work for and not write any more than that, even though it meant I spent half a year writing it. Otherwise I'd have been completely exhausted and never actually finished it!

PAPER 1 Reading and
Use of English

PAPER 2 Writing ▶ Part 1

Part 2

PAPER 3 Listening

PAPER 4 Speaking

You **must** answer this question. Write your answer in **140–190** words.

1 In your English class you have been talking about fast food. Now, your English teacher has asked you to write an essay.

Write an essay using **all** the notes and give reasons for your point of view.

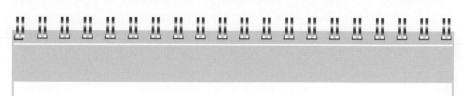

Is fast food always a bad thing?

Notes
Write about:

1. health
2. cost
3. .... (your own idea)

Write an answer to **one** of the questions **2–5** in this part. Write your answer in **140–190** words in an appropriate style.

2   You see this notice in an international magazine:

Can one day change your life?

Have the events on a single day had a major influence on your life?
Write about your experience, and say how it changed your life.

We will publish the best articles in our magazine.

Write your **article**.

3   You recently attended a performance of a play. Write a review for your college English-language magazine giving your own opinion of the play. Include information about the story, the acting, the sets and costumes.

Write your **review**.

4   (*for FIRST candidates only*)

The editor of your college English-language magazine is going to publish a special issue about part-time summer jobs for teenagers. You have been asked to write a report about a summer job you did, describing your job and explaining why it was a positive or negative experience.

Write your **report**.

(*for FIRST FOR SCHOOLS candidates only*)

You see this announcement in your school English-language magazine.

Stories wanted

Write a story for our magazine! Your story must begin with this sentence:

Nola knew that today would be a very special day.

Your story must include:
  • a journey
  • some friends

Write your **story**.

5   (*for FIRST FOR SCHOOLS candidates only*) Answer the following question based on your reading of one of the set books.

'The theme of a good book, the message we take away after reading it, must help us in our everyday lives.' Do you agree or disagree with this statement? Write an **essay**, giving your opinions with reference to the book or short story you have read.

◉ ▶ **Track 21**

You will hear people talking in eight different situations. For questions **1–8**, choose the best answer (**A**, **B** or **C**).

1   You hear a girl talking about a new film.
    Why does she want to see it?
    A   to have a better understanding of the novel it is based on
    B   because her friends have recommended it
    C   because she likes action films

2   You hear a man talking about a car journey he made recently.
    Where was the biggest traffic jam?
    A   coming out of London
    B   near the airport
    C   getting off the motorway

3   You hear a woman talking about a present.
    What was she given?
    A   a piece of clothing
    B   some jewellery
    C   a drawing

4   You hear a boy talking about his favourite footballer.
    Which team does he play for?
    A   Arsenal
    B   Liverpool
    C   Birmingham

5   You hear a man booking theatre tickets by phone.
    How much will they cost altogether?
    A   £73
    B   £75
    C   £78

6   You hear a woman talking about moving to Scotland.
    How did she feel when she met her neighbours?
    A   pleased they were so friendly
    B   annoyed because she couldn't understand their accent
    C   surprised that they treated her like a foreigner

7   You hear a radio advertisement for a museum.
    What period does the special exhibition deal with?
    A   the 1940s
    B   the 1920s
    C   the 1950s

8   You hear two friends talking about a television programme they have both seen
    What sort of programme was it?
    A   a quiz show
    B   a documentary
    C   a soap opera

🎧 **Track 22**

You will hear a talk by a man called Graham Jones, who designs model railways in Britain. For questions **9–18**, complete the sentences with a word or short phrase.

Model railways

In the 1980s and 1990s, models were considered to be

(**9**) ....

Britain is the (**10**) .... railway model market in Europe.

For parents, model railways are a (**11**) .... alternative
to computers and videogames.

Most people who buy model railway equipment nowadays are

(**12**) ....

Purchasers of model trains include lawyers, business executives and

(**13**) ....

Children will always be interested in toy models of

(**14**) .... objects.

Model railways will continue to appeal mainly to

(**15**) ....

Companies that make model railways are now investing in countries in

(**16**) ....

Manufacturers will be promoting their products at international

(**17**) ....

Model trains are available that are (**18**) ....
by computers.

PAPER 1 Reading and
Use of English

PAPER 2 Writing

PAPER 3 Listening

PAPER 4 Speaking

Part 1
Part 2
Part 3
Part 4

🔊 **Track 23**

You will hear five short extracts in which people are talking about their memories of their first day at school. For questions **19–23**, choose from the list (**A–H**) what each speaker remembers about the experience. Use the letters only once. There are three extra letters which you do not need to use.

A I was late for the first class.

B The building seemed very big.

Speaker 1 | 19

C A relative of mine was already there.

Speaker 2 | 20

D I felt very lonely.

Speaker 3 | 21

E I was glad there wasn't a uniform.

Speaker 4 | 22

F I wasn't wearing the right clothes.

Speaker 5 | 23

G I had to walk to school alone.

H I had a positive feeling from the very start.

Track 24

You will hear part of a radio interview with a law student called Mark Stone, talking about his life at university. For questions **24–30**, choose the best answer (**A**, **B** or **C**).

24 Why did Mark decide to study at Gramwell University?
   A It offers a very good course in his subject.
   B His parents advised him to go there.
   C It is near where he grew up.

25 When Mark arrived at Gramwell, he was surprised by
   A the weather.
   B the architecture.
   C the atmosphere.

26 What does Mark say about his studies?
   A It is difficult to manage his time well.
   B It is less demanding now than it used to be.
   C It is worth studying hard.

27 Why did Mark get a part-time job?
   A He wanted experience working as a librarian.
   B He had to cover the cost of his accommodation.
   C He was getting bored in his spare time.

28 What does Mark say about his lecturers?
   A They like to communicate with students.
   B They are hard to get to know.
   C They only occasionally want to see students.

29 What does Mark say about his friends at Gramwell?
   A Most people he knows study law.
   B They study a variety of different subjects.
   C The subjects they study are more interesting than law.

30 How does Mark feel about his social life?
   A He wishes he could go to more parties.
   B He worries about wasting time.
   C He believes he studies better after doing sport.

Part 1 (2 minutes)

The examiner (interlocutor) will ask each of you to speak briefly in turn and to give personal information about yourselves. You can expect a variety of questions, such as:

Who are the most important people in your life?
How many brothers and sisters do you have?
Do you have much contact with your aunts and uncles, cousins, etc.?
What do you most enjoy doing with your family?

Part 2 (4 minutes)

You will each be asked to talk for a minute without interruption. You will each be given two different photographs in turn to talk about. After your partner has finished speaking, you will be asked a brief question connected with your partner's photographs.

1 Painters

Look at the two photographs on page 174 which show painters and their work.

Candidate A, compare these photographs, and say which painting you like most and why.

Candidate B, which of these paintings do you prefer? (Why?)

2 Shops

Look at the two photographs on page 175 which show places where people shop.

Candidate B, compare these photographs, and say what the advantages of shopping in each place are.

Candidate A, which of these places would you prefer to shop in? (Why?)

Part 3 (4 minutes)

You will be asked to discuss something together without interruption by the examiner. You will have a page of ideas with a question to help you.

Holiday resorts

Imagine that a travel company is deciding on the best holiday resorts to include on its website. Turn to page 176 which shows different facilities and a question for you to discuss. Talk to each other about how important each facility is for visitors to a holiday resort. Then decide which two are the most important.

Part 4 (4 minutes)

The examiner will encourage you to develop the topic of your discussion in Part 3 by asking questions such as:

Would you prefer to spend a holiday in a small village or in a city? (Why?)
Would you prefer to go on holiday to somewhere cold or somewhere hot? (Why?)
Do you think school holidays are long enough in your country? (Why? / Why not?)
Do you think it's a good idea for teenagers to go away on holiday without their parents? (Why? / Why not?)
Where do people in your country like to go on holiday? (Why?)
What do most people in your country like to do while they're on holiday? (Why?)

PAPER 1 Reading and Use of English

▶▶ PART 5

refuge (n) a place where you can get away from unpleasant conditions

amid (prep) among

urban (adj) city

freight car (n) part of a train used for transporting goods

crumbling (adj) breaking into small pieces

tended (adj) looked after

vantage point (n) a place from which there is a clear view

cease (v) to stop

spark (v) to start

designate (v) to choose, appoint

▶▶ PART 6

equivalent (n) something that is the same

claim (v) to state that something is true, especially when there is some doubt

region (n) a part, a section

abstract (adj) unclear, vague

orientate (v) to find your position with a map

budget (n) an amount of money set aside for a purpose

recall (v) to remember something

acquisition (n) the act of getting new skills or knowledge

indication (n) a sign, a signal

coordinate (v) to harmonise

schedule (n) a list of timed, planned activities or events

▶▶ PART 7

biography (n) the history of a person's life

award (v) to give a prize (honour, praise, etc.) to someone

exhausted (adj) extremely tired

vow (v) to swear, to solemnly promise

frank (adj) open, direct, unafraid to express the truth

lucrative (adj) producing a lot of money, profitable

fiction (n) a type of literature based upon the author's imagination as opposed to true stories

gold rush (n) a rush of people to a place where gold has been discovered

publish (v) to print and distribute something to the public

draft (n) one version of something written

offend (v) to hurt the feelings of people

talk someone out of doing something (phr v) to discourage someone from doing something

intriguing (adj) interesting, fascinating, causing curiosity

hesitant (adj) unsure, reluctant

impetuous (adj) done quickly, often without thinking, impulsive

tie down (phr v) to restrict

PAPER 1 Reading and ▶ **Part 1**
        Use of English   Part 2
PAPER 2 Writing   Part 3
                           Part 4
PAPER 3 Listening   Part 5
PAPER 4 Speaking   Part 6
                           Part 7

For questions **1–8**, read the text below and decide which word (**A, B, C** or **D**) best fits each gap. There is an example at the beginning (**0**).

Mark your answers **on the separate answer sheet**.

Example:

0   **A**   mysterious   **B**   secret   **C**   hidden   **D**   confidential

0	**A**	**B**	**C**	**D**

The bobcat

Native to North America, the bobcat, sometimes called 'wildcat', is a (**0**) .... and nocturnal animal and is (**1**) .... seen by people. Bobcats are (**2**) .... twice the size of the average domestic cat. Most have a grey to brown coat and a short, black-tipped tail, which seems to be cut off or 'bobbed', hence its name. They have long legs, large paws, and tufted ears (**3**) .... to those of their larger relative, the Canada lynx.

Bobcats roam (**4**) .... much of North America and are able to adapt to such (**5**) .... habitats as deserts, forests, swamps, and have even been seen in suburban areas. On the rare occasion that these solitary animals are spotted, they are usually (**6**) .... Females tend to find quiet, undisturbed dens to (**7**) .... a litter of one to six kittens, which will stay with their mother for between nine months and a year, when they will learn to hunt before finally (**8**) .... out on their own.

1	**A** almost	**B** rarely	**C** little	**D** slightly
2	**A** greatly	**B** considerably	**C** roughly	**D** relatively
3	**A** same	**B** similar	**C** like	**D** as
4	**A** throughout	**B** during	**C** near	**D** among
5	**A** many	**B** mixed	**C** various	**D** diverse
6	**A** individual	**B** lonely	**C** separate	**D** alone
7	**A** rise	**B** grow	**C** raise	**D** provide
8	**A** setting	**B** being	**C** leaving	**D** entering

PAPER 1 Reading and ▸
Use of English
PAPER 2 Writing
PAPER 3 Listening
PAPER 4 Speaking

Part 1
Part 2
Part 3
Part 4
Part 5
Part 6
Part 7

For questions **9–16**, read the text below and think of the word which best fits each gap. Use only **one** word in each gap. There is an example at the beginning (**0**).

Write your answers **IN CAPITAL LETTERS on the separate answer sheet.**

Example: | 0 | O N E | | | | | | | | | | | | | | | | | | | | | | |

The origin of our language

Sir William Jones, born in 1746, was undoubtedly (**0**) .... of the greatest linguists who ever lived. He had an amazing talent (**9**) .... languages and learnt several at a young age. (**10**) .... the time of his death, he had a thorough knowledge of 13 languages and knowledge of a further 28.

Apart (**11**) .... studying languages, he also studied law and became a judge in India. He was fascinated by this vast subcontinent and wrote about Indian life. He also translated important works of Indian literature.

Jones noticed (**12**) .... Sanskrit, a classical Indian language, was similar to Greek and Latin in a number of ways. The resemblance (**13**) .... not be a coincidence. Several other people (**14**) .... also noted similarities, but Jones was (**15**) .... first to suggest that these three languages had a common origin. He also suggested that they could be grouped together with other European and Asian languages into one family, known (**16**) .... Indo-European languages, which included English.

PAPER 1 Reading and ▸ Part 1
        Use of English   Part 2
                            Part 3
PAPER 2 Writing   Part 4
                            Part 5
PAPER 3 Listening   Part 6
PAPER 4 Speaking   Part 7

For questions **17–24**, read the text below. Use the word given in capitals at the end of some of the lines to form a word that fits in the gap **in the same line**. There is an example at the beginning (**0**).

Write your answers **IN CAPITAL LETTERS on the separate answer sheet.**

Example: | 0 | P | O | P | U | L | A | T | I | O | N | | | | | | | |

Left-handedness

Ten per cent of the (**0**) …….. is left-handed. Traditionally, there	**POPULATE**
has been a lot of social (**17**) …….. against left-handed people.	**DISCRIMINATE**
How hard is it for them to live in a right-handed world?	
A number of (**18**) …….. items such as scissors have been	**PRACTICE**
(**19**) …….. for right-handed people. It can be very	**DESIGN**
(**20**) …….. for 'lefties' to be sitting next to 'righties' during	**CONVENIENT**
dinner. Commonly-used computer keys are on the right	
of the keyboard. Lefties have to use their own sports	
(**21**) …….. . Less frequently-used car controls such as	**EQUIP**
headlight switches are also on the right.	
Forcing children to use their right hand can cause	
(**22**) …….. at school, which may then have an impact on	**DIFFICULT**
left-handed students' academic (**23**) …….. . It can also result	**DEVELOP**
in learning problems like dyslexia. Trying to make lefties	
use their right hand can explain potentially rebellious	
(**24**) …….. at school, as well as causing clumsiness	**BEHAVE**
and frustration.	

For questions **25–30**, complete the second sentence so that it has a similar meaning to the first sentence, using the word given. **Do not change the word given.** You must use between **two** and **five** words, including the word given. Here is an example (**0**).

Example:

0   I'll be very happy when I go on holiday.

FORWARD

I'm .... on holiday.

The gap can be filled by the words 'looking forward to going' so you write:

Example: | 0 | LOOKING FORWARD TO GOING |

Write only the missing words **IN CAPITAL LETTERS on the separate answer sheet**.

---

25   The village is the same as it was in the 1950s.

CHANGED

The village .... the 1950s.

26   Our cat was sleeping on the sofa all afternoon.

SPENT

Our cat .... on the sofa.

27   It was so hot that she fainted.

IF

She .... it hadn't been so hot.

28   I enjoy watching football more than motor racing.

RATHER

I .... motor racing.

29   Please reply immediately on receipt of this notification.

SOON

Please reply .... this notification.

30   The coffee machine in our office hasn't worked for three months.

OUT

The coffee machine in our office .... for three months.

PAPER 1	Reading and Use of English ▶	Part 1
		Part 2
PAPER 2	Writing	Part 3
		Part 4
PAPER 3	Listening	**Part 5**
PAPER 4	Speaking	Part 6
		Part 7

You are going to read part of a story about a mountain climber. For questions **31–36**, choose the answer (**A**, **B**, **C** or **D**) which you think fits best according to the text.

Mark your answers **on the separate answer sheet**.

A steep learning curve

Journalist Dan Greenbaum abandons his laptop and learns how to climb

Living in an area of the country where there's little more than a slight incline to stroll up on the way to the shops, the highest climb I'd ever done was up the stairs to bed. As a writer on an adventure sports magazine, I'd always fought shy of doing the adventurous stuff myself, preferring instead to observe the experts from a safe distance and relay their experiences to readers in the form of prose. So, when I was challenged to take part in a mountain climb in aid of raising money for charity – and to write about it afterwards – I was unwilling to say the least.

Despite their awe-inspiring strength and agility, even experienced climbers fail to make climbing look simple. I knew a mammoth task lay before me if I was to get into even half-decent physical shape before the four thousand-metre climb, which would involve sheer rock faces and steep, snow-covered terrain. I set about consuming not only energy-boosting food to help me get through my intense training regime, but also devouring every climbing magazine I could get my hands on.

I was lucky enough to have a brilliant climbing coach called Keith, who put me through my paces after the daily grind at the keyboard was over. My mentor imparted keen knowledge about everything from the importance of building specific muscle groups to how to combat fatigue through nutrition. I listened, speechless, while he went into great detail about everything to do with the sport. It quickly became apparent that the mechanics of climbing were more complex than I could have imagined. And there wasn't only the strength and endurance-building to contend with, but the gear, too. I had to get to grips with an array of equipment and techniques I'd never even heard of: 'crampons', 'glissade' and 'self-arrest', all of which I learned would come in handy on the snow-capped peak I'd be ascending in a few months' time.

line 21   Aware of the challenge that lay ahead, Keith made a detailed action plan and I forced myself to stick to it diligently, doing a daily workout at the gym, eating carbohydrates, and going on long hikes with a heavy backpack. I perfected my technique on the climbing wall and even squeezed in a weekend away to the Scottish mountains to get in some vital experience of trekking through snow and ice. My self-belief increased alongside my muscle power and I became not only confident about finishing the climb, but determined to do it with flying colours.

All too soon I was on a plane to my destination – Switzerland. Early one clear spring morning I peered out of a hostel window and up at the mountain I would attempt to ascend that day. My hard-won confidence took a nose dive as the enormity of what I'd let myself in for struck me as suddenly as an avalanche: I sank down on my bed and for a brief moment considered fleeing. And then I remembered all the hard work I'd done to get here and how disappointed Keith would be if I ducked out at the last minute – not to mention letting down the charity and the sense of failure I'd experience myself. With a deep breath I tied my boot laces, gathered my gear and headed out to into the sunshine to meet the rest of the group.

And as I sit here now, tapping away on my laptop, with the ordeal safely behind me, I'm amazed at the detail in which I can recall every second of the climb; the burning muscles, the sheer exhaustion, the minor setbacks along the way. Could I have been better prepared? Possibly. Would I be back for another go? Thankfully not. The exhilaration of standing on top of the world is a never-to-be-repeated experience, but one I will cherish forever nonetheless.

31 In the first paragraph, the writer reveals his

- **A** difficulty in accurately recounting the stories of expert sportspeople.
- **B** disappointment in the exercise opportunities available in his town.
- **C** lack of interest in listening to professional climbers' personal tales.
- **D** lack of enthusiasm for the challenge he'd been offered.

32 In the second paragraph, we know that the writer is

- **A** keen to learn as much about mountain climbing as he is able to.
- **B** worried that he won't have time to prepare well enough for the climb.
- **C** amazed by how easy professional climbers make the activity seem.
- **D** concerned about the difficulty of climbing in certain conditions.

33 What do we learn in the third paragraph?

- **A** The coach makes the writer realise how complicated climbing is.
- **B** The writer doesn't think he'll be able to cope with the equipment he needs to use.
- **C** The writer is confused by the information about food that the coach gives him.
- **D** The coach doesn't believe the writer is doing enough work towards his climb.

34 What does 'it' refer to in line 21?

- **A** a daily workout at the gym
- **B** the challenge
- **C** a detailed action plan
- **D** the writer's coach

35 How does the writer use the example of an avalanche in the fifth paragraph?

- **A** to highlight a strong and unexpected feeling
- **B** to explain the way he sat down on his bed
- **C** to describe what he could see from his window
- **D** to emphasize how quickly he wanted to run away

36 How does the writer feel looking back on his climb?

- **A** satisfied that he had done his best
- **B** relieved that he wouldn't have to do it again
- **C** surprised that he had managed to complete it
- **D** regretful that it hadn't gone as smoothly as it could have

PAPER 1 Reading and
          Use of English

PAPER 2 Writing

PAPER 3 Listening

PAPER 4 Speaking

Part 1
Part 2
Part 3
Part 4
Part 5
Part 6
Part 7

You are going to read a newspaper article about a pirate radio station. Six sentences have been removed from the article. Choose from the sentences **A–G** the one which fits each gap (**37–42**). There is one extra sentence, which you do not need to use.

Mark your answers **on the separate answer sheet**.

Pirate radio stations

In 1964, a radio station on a boat off the coast of Britain began broadcasting pop music. Radio Caroline's style was young and fresh – and the station itself was outside British law.

The British government now grants licences for people to operate radio and TV stations, but in the 1960s the only radio stations that existed legally in Britain were run by the BBC, the state-owned broadcasting company, and the government would not allow anyone to operate a private radio station. **37** The Irishman who founded Radio Caroline simply put the radio equipment on a boat and anchored it just outside the three-mile limit.

Why would anyone go to so much trouble to start up a radio station? One reason was the BBC's policy on the kind of music it broadcast. During a period when pop music was extremely popular, the BBC played very little of it on its radio stations. It was felt that the BBC should cater for more conservative tastes in music. **38** It was only a matter of time before an enterprising businessman who managed some pop music bands realised that here was a huge potential market.

There was, in fact, a radio station operating outside Britain at the time transmitting programmes that could be received in the country: Radio Luxembourg. **39** It was only after Radio Caroline went on the air that people were able to listen to pop music broadcast in English all day.

As well as playing the sort of music that young people liked, Radio Caroline was popular with listeners for other reasons. The disc jockeys didn't have the typical BBC pronunciation, which was considered by many to be formal and old-fashioned. Instead they spoke with regional accents, they used colloquial English, they were cheeky and informal. Audiences loved it and soon large numbers of listeners were tuning in.

Then other pirate radio stations began to spring up and the British government decided that some action had to be taken. **40** However, it soon became clear that the authorities were being forced to face the new situation created by the pirate radio stations. These had shown that pop music was here to stay, and that young people desperately wanted to listen to radio stations that played it.

Was there a lesson to be learnt from all this? Indeed there was! The BBC decided to start up its own pop music radio station, Radio 1, and before long Radio Caroline disc jockeys were working there. **41**

In a further development, the British government decided to allow commercial radio stations to operate in the country. This meant stations could now do legally what Radio Caroline had been doing illegally – and in far more comfortable conditions. **42** Its situation became even worse when the ship from which it was operating sank. The crew and disc jockeys had to be rescued.

Today Radio Caroline still exists although it is no longer as popular as it was in the 1960s. But it made history by forcing the BBC to change its policy on pop music and the nature of its relationship with its listeners.

A The radio station went on to become a legend, and its disc jockeys won fame and fortune.

B Not surprisingly, Radio Caroline found itself in serious financial difficulties.

C As a result, there were large numbers of young people who wanted to listen to a particular type of music, but couldn't.

D What is more, increasing numbers of listeners were switching from the pirate stations to the eminent broadcaster.

E But this station used to play only a short section of each song – and this was clearly not satisfactory.

F However, the government's power only extended to the country itself and the seas around it up to around five kilometres from the shore.

G In 1967, a new law was passed making it illegal to advertise or supply an offshore radio station from the UK.

You are going to read an article in which four people talk about their experiences of playing a musical instrument. For questions **43–52**, choose from the people (**A–D**). The people may be chosen more than once.

Mark your answers **on the separate answer sheet**.

Which person

mentions other people's reluctance to do what's required?	**43**
mentions an initial confidence in their ability?	**44**
experienced indirect musical input from others?	**45**
says that a certain belief is relevant to other activities?	**46**
recognises a particular advantage of studying music?	**47**
proved another person right?	**48**
had an unexpected understanding of what they were trying to do?	**49**
prefers to keep their skills to themselves?	**50**
is keen to disprove a particular opinion?	**51**
wanted to fulfil someone else's wish?	**52**

Musical magic

A Andrea Beecham

I play the bass guitar in a band. Everyone assumes that it's just one of those teenage things – something I'll get bored with or grow out of. They reckon I'm just in it because I want to be famous but nothing could be further from the truth. Sure, the money would be fantastic, but I'd rather not experience being recognised everywhere you go. The reality is that I just love performing, and striving to produce something that other people want to listen to. You've got to be patient and persevere and practise, practise, practise if you want to get any better at an instrument – which I think a lot of people tend to overlook. That's why they tend to give up before they've even started. I guess you could apply that same principle to lots of things – you only get out what you put in.

B Mike Tindale

I wouldn't say I had any particular desire to learn an instrument, but when I was about eight my parents insisted I give it a go. They'd both turned down the chance to learn the piano when they were younger because they thought it looked like hard work, and they both regretted their decision. So I went along to my first lesson just to keep them happy. To my surprise, I took to it really quickly and was keen to get ahead. I still play now and, although I'll let my own kids decide for themselves whether they want to take up an instrument or not, I've noticed there are some benefits to keeping your mind active in this way. I like to think I have pretty good coordination skills, which I put down to learning an instrument that requires you to use both hands, both feet and engage your brain simultaneously!

C Dave Warwick

I remember hearing someone play the violin on the radio when I was little and that was it! I pestered my dad to let me have some lessons, and he was happy to indulge me in what he thought was just another phase. We hired an instrument from a local music shop and I went along brimming with enthusiasm and excitement to my first lesson, convinced I was about to become a famous musician. More fool me! I was shocked by the awful scraping sound which I produced and suddenly realised what I'd let myself in for. This was going to be no easy task and it would be a very long time before I'd come close to the beautiful singing violin I'd heard on the radio. I never went back. Do I regret not sticking it out? Maybe. But I think I'd rather listen to the professional musicians. I know they do it so much better than I ever could.

D Maria Perez

I'm pretty shy when it comes to getting up on stage and showing people what I can do on my drum kit, even though my friends are always really encouraging. I've been messing about on drums as far back as I can remember – my mum plays them, so there was always a kit in the house. I never had any formal training, I'd just pick up the rhythms I heard Mum play and then imitate them. I'm glad I grew up in such a creative environment – there were always loads of other musicians hanging around the house when I was a kid and some of them were pretty inspirational. It's just that performing isn't really my thing – I've only ever played the drums for my own amusement, rather than intending to make a career out of it.

You **must** answer this question. Write your answer in **140–190** words in an appropriate style.

1 In your English class you have been talking about fashion. Now, your English teacher has asked you to write an essay.

Write an essay using **all** the notes and give reasons for your point of view.

It's important to wear the latest fashions. Do you agree?

Notes
Write about:

1. cost
2. your image
3. .... (your own idea)

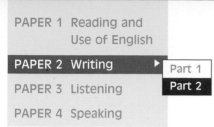
Write an answer to **one** of the questions 2–5 in this part. Write your answer in **140–190** words in an appropriate style.

2   This is part of an email from your English-speaking friend.

> Thanks very much for inviting me to stay with you and your family last weekend. It was fun! Would you like to stay with me and my family for a weekend next month? What would you like to do? Is there anything you can't eat?
>
> Write soon!
>
> Li

Write your **email**.

3   You recently saw this notice in an English-language magazine called *Young Film Critic*:

> **WANTED: GREAT FILMS WITH GREAT STORIES**
>
> Films can rely too much on special effects instead of a good story or good acting. Write a review of a film that used many special effects. How good or bad was the film? Did it rely too heavily on special effects?
>
> We'll publish the best reviews next month!

Write your **review**.

4   (*for FIRST candidates only*)

Your teacher has asked you to write a report about what facilities there are for young people in your local area. Describe what facilities are available and explain whether they are suitable for young people's needs. Suggest what other facilities young people might like to have.

Write your **report**.

(*for FIRST FOR SCHOOLS candidates only*) You see this announcement in an English-language magazine for teenagers.

> **Stories wanted**
>
> We are looking for stories for our magazine. Your story must begin with this sentence:
>
> *If I had known what was going to happen, I would never have made that phone call.*
>
> Your story must include:
> • a bus journey
> • a stranger you meet

Write your **story**.

5   (*for FIRST FOR SCHOOLS candidates only*) Answer the following question based on your reading of **one** of the set books.

'If a story is good, it doesn't matter where and when it is set. Good stories have universal appeal.' Do you agree or disagree with this statement? Write an **essay**, giving your opinions with reference to the book or short story you have read.

Track 25

You will hear people talking in eight different situations. For questions **1–8**, choose the best answer (**A**, **B** or **C**).

1 You hear two school friends talking about a drumming workshop they will take part in.
   How does the boy feel about it?
   A worried that he won't understand what to do
   B excited by the prospect of learning something new
   C nervous about a particular part of it

2 You hear a woman talking about a shopping trip.
   What does she say about it?
   A She fulfilled the original aim of the trip.
   B She spent more than she had intended to.
   C She had planned what to buy herself in advance.

3 You hear a man talking about a car he used to own.
   Why did he decide to sell it?
   A because he wanted to economise
   B because he no longer needed it
   C because he needed a more comfortable car

4 You hear a woman phoning the reception desk of her hotel.
   What is the problem with her room?
   A The heating doesn't work.
   B The television is out of order.
   C The door doesn't close properly.

5 You hear a girl talking to her father about a school trip.
   What is her father concerned about?
   A The activities may not be interesting for the students.
   B The students might spend too much time alone.
   C The trip will cost more than he can afford.

6 You hear a man describing a trip in a hot-air balloon.
   How did he feel when the balloon started to rise?
   A astonished at the silence around him
   B nervous because the basket was not steady
   C worried that they would drift out of control

7 You hear two friends talking about an exercise routine.
   What do they agree about?
   A how unlikely it is to work
   B how easy it must be to maintain
   C how tiring it sounds

8 You hear a woman talking about a magazine she used to read as a teenager.
   What did she like most about it?
   A the fashion tips
   B the interviews with pop stars
   C the stories

🎧 **Track 26**

You will hear part of a presentation by a woman called Linda Brown, who is the director of a new college. For questions **9–18**, complete the sentences with a word or short phrase.

Woodley community college

Summer school classes start on (**9**) ....

People expressed interest in the college after several

(**10**) .... were broadcast on the radio.

The (**11**) .... will declare the college open.

Other figures at the opening ceremony, include a famous

(**12**) .... , who will make a speech.

Local (**13**) .... will teach courses at the college.

The emphasis will be on (**14**) .... subjects.

The college will be (**15**) .... about who it allows to enrol for courses.

Students may not have the (**16**) .... required by traditional colleges.

It is hoped that an (**17**) .... office in the city centre will generate interest in the college.

People interested in courses should first refer to its

(**18**) .... for more information.

PAPER 1   Reading and
              Use of English

PAPER 2   Writing

PAPER 3   Listening ▶

PAPER 4   Speaking

Part 1
Part 2
Part 3
Part 4

Track 27

You will hear five short extracts in which people are describing what they like most about the city of New York in the USA. For questions **19–23**, choose from the list (**A–H**) the reason each speaker gives for why the city appeals to them. Use the letters only once. There are three extra letters which you do not need to use.

A   There are plenty of sightseeing opportunities.

B   It has a mixture of ethnicities.

C   It is a fantastic place for shopping.

D   The local people have a great sense of humour.

E   It's a very energetic and lively place.

F   The architecture is very impressive.

G   There's a wide choice of places to eat.

H   The museums and galleries are fascinating.

Speaker 1	19
Speaker 2	20
Speaker 3	21
Speaker 4	22
Speaker 5	23

PAPER 1 Reading and
         Use of English

PAPER 2 Writing

PAPER 3 Listening ▶
                          | Part 1
                          | Part 2
                          | Part 3
                          | **Part 4**

PAPER 4 Speaking

Track 28

You will hear an interview with a man called Ray Garrett, who is a professional deep-sea diver. For questions **24–30**, choose the best answer (**A**, **B** or **C**).

24 Ray became a deep-sea diver because he
    A lost his job as an office manager.
    B didn't enjoy working in an office.
    C had worked as a diving instructor.

25 What did Ray's parents think of his new career?
    A They knew he didn't have enough experience to do the course.
    B They thought that he wouldn't be able to complete the course.
    C They believed that he didn't have the strength to do the course.

26 Most of the work that Ray does
    A is boring but completely safe.
    B keeps him underwater for over two hours.
    C is not in very deep water.

27 According to Ray, accidents happen when divers
    A dive down to the sea bed.
    B work on shipwrecks at the bottom of the sea.
    C forget to think about possible dangers.

28 At the moment, Ray
    A is repairing a ship in America.
    B is working on a ship that sank off the coast of America.
    C is looking for a ship that sank 150 ago.

29 What does Ray say about the ship, the SS Union?
    A It was travelling to the northern states when it sank.
    B It might have been carrying a valuable cargo.
    C It sank towards the beginning of the twentieth century.

30 According to Ray, if a shipwreck breaks up, a diver
    A might be unable to return to the surface.
    B might suffer from air embolism.
    C might have to dive too deep.

Part 1 (2 minutes)

The examiner (interlocutor) will ask each of you to speak briefly in turn and to give personal information about yourselves. You can expect a variety of questions, such as:

Are you a student or do you work?
What do you enjoy about what you do? (Why?)
What are your plans for the future?
What do you think is the ideal job? (Why?)

Part 2 (4 minutes)

You will each be asked to talk for a minute without interruption. You will each be given two different photographs in turn to talk about. After your partner has finished speaking, you will be asked a brief question connected with your partner's photographs.

1 Special moments

Look at the two photographs on page 177 which show people enjoying special moments in their lives.

Candidate A, compare these photographs, and say what makes these moments special for these people.

Candidate B, which of these do you think is more memorable? (Why?)

2 Climates

Look at the two photographs on page 178 which show different types of climate.

Candidate B, compare these photographs, and say what you think it would be like to live in each of these climates.

Candidate A, which climate would you prefer to live in? (Why?)

Part 3 (4 minutes)

You will be asked to discuss something together without interruption by the examiner. You will have a page of ideas and a question to help you.

Evening and weekend classes

Imagine your local college intends to run some evening and weekend classes. Turn to page 179 which shows some classes that could be offered and a question for you to discuss. Talk to each other about how each class might attract different people. Then decide which two of the classes you think should be offered by the college.

Part 4 (4 minutes)

The examiner will encourage you to develop the topic of your discussion in Part 3 by asking questions such as:

What other classes do you think people might enjoy taking? (Why?)
Why do you think people attend classes outside of school or work?
Why do you think some people don't like to learn new things?
Do you think schools and colleges should offer classes in the evenings or weekends? (Why? / Why not?)
What sort of subjects would you like to learn about? (Why?)
What benefits are there of doing activities which are different from work or schoolwork?

PAPER 1 Reading and Use of English

▶▶ PART 5

hut (n) a small dwelling of simple construction, especially one made of natural materials

livid (adj) dark bluish grey

loosen (v) to make or become less tight or firm

grip (v) to grasp or seize firmly, to hold fast

tumble (v) to fall

face (n) a steep, high side of a mountain

awkward (adj) difficult

despise (v) to hate, to detest

haul (v) to pull slowly and with difficulty

bound (v) to jump

cannon (v) to knock into someone or something

hum (v) to make a continuous sound

gaze (v) to look at something for a long time

skip (v) to run in a hopping way

overhanging (adj) sticking out over

canopy (n) a cover

thump (n) the sound of a heavy object when it hits the ground

tug (v) to pull hard

clamp (v) to hold something tightly

arch (v) to form a curved shape

crush (v) to press something so hard that it breaks

hoop (n) a circular tube

snatch (v) to take something quickly, to grab, to seize

sideways (adv) to one side

mountaineer (n) a mountain guide or person who climbs mountains for fun

▶▶ PART 6

grant (v) to allow someone to have something that they have asked for

found (v) to start something such as an organisation or school

anchor (v) to lower a piece of heavy metal to the bottom of the sea to prevent a ship from moving

policy (n) a way of doing something that has been officially agreed by an organisation

cater for (phr v) to provide a particular group of people with the things they need or want

conservative (adj) traditional

enterprising (adj) having the ability to think of new ideas and make them work

transmit (v) to send out electronic signals, etc. using radio, television or other equipment

regional accent (phr) a way of pronouncing words, which shows that you do not come from the capital city, but from a particular part of the country

colloquial (adj) of language, used mainly in informal conversations

cheeky (adj) rude or disrespectful in a way that is amusing

tune in (phr v) to listen to a broadcast on radio

spring up (phr v) to appear suddenly, to start to exist suddenly

switch (v) to change from doing one thing to doing another

eminent (adj) famous, important and respected

extend (v) to affect

▶▶ PART 7

assume (v) to think that something is true, without question or proof

strive (v) to try very hard to do or achieve something

persevere (v) to keep trying

principle (n) basic idea

desire (n) a strong feeling you want to do something

turn down (phr v) to refuse an offer or request

take to something (phr v) to like and learn a new skill

benefit (n) an advantage

simultaneously (adv) at the same time

pester (v) to ask repeatedly in an annoying way

indulge (v) to let someone do what they want

phase (n) a stage or period

brimming (adj) full

stick something out (v) to continue to do something to the end

imitate (v) to copy

PAPER 1 Reading and ▶ Part 1
         Use of English   Part 2
PAPER 2 Writing   Part 3
                            Part 4
PAPER 3 Listening   Part 5
PAPER 4 Speaking   Part 6
                            Part 7

For questions **1–8**, read the text below and decide which word (**A, B, C** or **D**) best fits each gap. There is an example at the beginning (**0**).

Mark your answers **on the separate answer sheet**.

Example:

| 0 | **A** huge | **B** vast | **C** large | **D** immense |

```
0 | A   B   C   D
    ‾   ▬   ‾   ‾
```

The old gate

In the Middle Ages the (**0**) .... majority of European cities had walls around them. They (**1**) .... to defend the city, but they also kept out undesirable people, like those with contagious (**2**) ....

Most of London's gates had been (**3**) .... by the end of the eighteenth century. However, by a (**4**) .... of luck, the last of them was preserved. This gate is, in (**5**) .... fact, not called a gate at all; its name is Temple Bar, and it marked the (**6**) .... between the old City of London and Westminster. However, as the (**7**) .... of traffic through London increased, Temple Bar became an obstacle to its free flow. In 1878 it was decided to take it down, so its stones were numbered, dismantled and put in (**8**) ....

In the 1970s the Temple Bar Trust was set up with the intention of returning the gate to the City of London. Today, Temple Bar stands next to St Paul's Cathedral.

1	**A** supposed	**B** served	**C** expected	**D** meant
2	**A** injuries	**B** symptoms	**C** wounds	**D** diseases
3	**A** devoted	**B** demolished	**C** deleted	**D** decreased
4	**A** stroke	**B** wave	**C** hit	**D** blow
5	**A** real	**B** current	**C** actual	**D** definite
6	**A** division	**B** part	**C** line	**D** boundary
7	**A** bulk	**B** quantity	**C** amount	**D** number
8	**A** storage	**B** store	**C** storeroom	**D** stock

For questions **9–16,** read the text below and think of the word which best fits each gap. Use only **one** word in each gap. There is an example at the beginning (**0**).

Write your answers **IN CAPITAL LETTERS on the separate answer sheet.**

Example: 0 | O | F |

Learning the language

Illiteracy is the condition (**0**) .... being unable to read and write. Illiteracy is also used (**9**) .... describe the condition of being ignorant in a particular subject or field. Computer illiteracy is (**10**) .... we call the inability to use a computer programming language.

Most of us (**11**) .... use computers can send emails, or know (**12**) .... to create a new folder. But we know almost (**13**) .... about programming languages, the artificial languages used to write instructions that can be executed by a computer. Only a very small percentage of computer users are able to read or write (**14**) .... kind of computer language. Should we make the effort to learn computer languages, especially when (**15**) .... are so complicated?

The answer is yes. Because of computer illiteracy, users are (**16**) .... the mercy of software manufacturers. Our society has become dependent on information technology, and this will no doubt be a problem for us for years to come.

PAPER 1	Reading and	▶	Part 1
	Use of English		Part 2
PAPER 2	Writing		**Part 3**
			Part 4
PAPER 3	Listening		Part 5
PAPER 4	Speaking		Part 6
			Part 7

For questions **17–24**, read the text below. Use the word given in capitals at the end of some of the lines to form a word that fits in the gap **in the same line**. There is an example at the beginning (**0**).

Write your answers **IN CAPITAL LETTERS on the separate answer sheet.**

Example: | **0** | A | S | S | O | C | I | A | T | I | O | N | S | | | | | | |

Film festivals

Film festivals are events staged by private organisations, local   **ASSOCIATE**
governments, arts (**0**) .... or film societies. They provide an   **KNOW**
opportunity for both famous and (**17**) .... film-makers to
present their movies to a real live audience and to have them
reviewed by (**18**) .... critics.   **PROFESSION**

Some festivals welcome a wide range of films, but other
festivals are more specialised. They may accept only comedies,
or only films made by female (**19**) .... Most festivals accept   **DIRECT**
submissions from any film maker, regardless of his or her
past experience.

Each festival has its own set of rules. (**20**) .... , film-makers   **GENERAL**
are given a deadline by which they have to submit their films.
Submitting a film to the wrong festival is likely to end in
(**21**) .... However, if a movie is accepted, the organisers   **REJECT**
(**22**) .... the film-maker. Film festivals are (**23**) ....   **NOTE**
divided into categories like drama, documentary   **TYPICAL**
or animation. Films are judged for their production value,
(**24**) .... and overall impression.   **CREATE**

PAPER 1	Reading and Use of English ▶	Part 1
		Part 2
		Part 3
		Part 4
PAPER 2	Writing	Part 5
PAPER 3	Listening	Part 6
PAPER 4	Speaking	Part 7

For questions **25–30**, complete the second sentence so that it has a similar meaning to the first sentence, using the word given. **Do not change the word given.** You must use between **two** and **five** words, including the word given. Here is an example (**0**).

Example:

0 I'll be very happy when I go on holiday.

FORWARD

I'm .... on holiday.

The gap can be filled by the words 'looking forward to going' so you write:

Example: | **0** | LOOKING FORWARD TO GOING |

Write **only** the missing words **IN CAPITAL LETTERS on the separate answer sheet**.

---

25 You've got to decide what you really want to do with your life.

TIME

It's .... what you really want to do with your life.

26 Each month he goes to the local hairdresser's for a haircut.

HAIR

Each month he .... at the local hairdresser's.

27 It was a mistake for you to insult Sarah.

SHOULD

You .... Sarah.

28 I'm sure Chris hasn't forgotten about the meeting.

HAVE

Chris .... about the meeting.

29 It's a pity we don't have a bigger apartment!

ONLY

If .... a bigger apartment!

30 The doctor told me to reduce the amount of sugar in my diet.

CUT

The doctor told me .... the amount of sugar in my diet.

PAPER 1 Reading and
         Use of English
PAPER 2 Writing
PAPER 3 Listening
PAPER 4 Speaking

Part 1
Part 2
Part 3
Part 4
Part 5
Part 6
Part 7

You are going to read part of an article about a pilot. For questions **31–36**, choose the answer (**A**, **B**, **C** or **D**) which you think fits best according to the text.

Mark your answers **on the separate answer sheet**.

Flying high

Barrington Irving is very good at rising above obstacles. Literally. Raised in Miami's inner city, surrounded by crime, poverty and failing schools, he beat the odds to become the youngest person ever to fly solo around the world. He built a plane himself, made his historic flight, graduated with excellent marks from an aeronautical science programme, and founded a dynamic educational non-profit-making organisation.
line 5   Then he turned 28.

His message for kids: 'The only thing that separates you from chief executives in corner offices or scientists in labs is determination, hard work, and a passion for what you want to achieve. The only person who can stop you from doing something great is you. Even if no one believes in your dream, you have to pursue it.' The secret, he believes, is having a dream in the first place, and that starts with powerful learning experiences that inspire kids to pursue careers – particularly in science, technology, engineering, and mathematics.

The moment of inspiration for Irving came at the age of 15 while he was working in his parents' bookstore. One of their customers, a Jamaican-born professional pilot, asked Irving if he'd ever thought about becoming a pilot. 'I told him I didn't think I was smart enough; but the next day he gave me the chance to sit in the cockpit of the commercial airplane he flew, and just like that I was hooked. There are probably millions of kids out there like me who find science and exploration amazing, but lack the confidence or opportunity to take the next step.'

To follow his dream, Irving turned down a full football scholarship to the University of Florida. He washed airplanes to earn money for flight school and increased his flying skills by practising at home on a $40 flight simulator video game. Then another dream took hold: flying solo around the world. He faced more than 50 rejections for sponsorship before convincing several manufacturers to donate individual aircraft components. He took off with no weather radar, no de-icing system, and just $30 in his pocket. 'I like to do things people say I can't do.'

After 97 days, 26 stops and dozens of thunderstorms, monsoons, snowstorms and sandstorms, he touched down to a roaring crowd in Miami. 'Stepping from the plane, it wasn't all the fanfare that changed my life. It was seeing so many young people watching and listening. I had no money, but I was determined to give back with my time, knowledge and experience.' He's been doing it ever since. Irving's non-profit-making organisation, Experience Aviation, aims to boost the numbers of youth in aviation and other science- and maths-related careers. Kids attend summer- and after-school programmes tackling hands-on robotics projects, flight simulator challenges and field trips to major industries and corporations. In his Build and Soar programme, 60 students from failing schools built an airplane from scratch in just ten weeks and then watched Irving pilot it into the clouds.

'We want to create a one-of-a-kind opportunity for students to take ownership and accomplish something amazing,' he notes. 'Meaningful, real-world learning experiences fire up the neurons in kids' minds. If you don't do that, you've lost them. Purposeful, inspiring activities increase the chance they'll stay on that learning and career path. We've had one young lady receive a full scholarship to Duke University to study mathematics, and several young men are now pilots, engineers, and aircraft mechanics.' Perhaps Irving's
line 39   most compelling educational tool is the example his own life provides. After landing his record-breaking flight at age 23, he smiled out at the airfield crowd and said, 'Everyone told me what I couldn't do. They said I was too young, that I didn't have enough money, experience, strength, or knowledge. They told me it would take forever and I'd never come home. Well ... guess what?'

31 Why does the writer say 'Then he turned 28' in line 5?

    A   to explain why Irving was ready for a change in his lifestyle
    B   to emphasise how much Irving had achieved in his life so far
    C   to show why Irving's organisation had become so successful
    D   to justify the enthusiasm Irving demonstrated through his actions

32 According to Irving, what is the most important requirement for success?

    A   having friends who believe you will eventually succeed
    B   having something specific that you want to accomplish
    C   having plenty of opportunities to study different subjects
    D   having contacts in organisations who can share their knowledge

33 What does Irving say about what happened in his parents' bookshop?

    A   He realised immediately how lucky he was.
    B   He felt too embarrassed to refuse the offer.
    C   He was initially doubtful about his own abilities.
    D   He understood that his efforts would be rewarded.

34 What do we learn about Irving in the fourth paragraph?

    A   Once he knew how to fly he took on a further challenge.
    B   He chose to get by on as low a budget as possible.
    C   He was eventually given just enough money to keep going.
    D   The most useful flying tips he picked up were from a game he bought.

35 Why did Irving set up his non profit making organisation?

    A   He wanted to help improve the schools in his area.
    B   He hoped to avoid becoming a celebrity pilot.
    C   He thought he could teach people more than the flight schools could.
    D   He saw there was widespread interest in what he was doing.

36 What does 'compelling' mean in line 39?

    A   exciting and demanding
    B   interesting and amusing
    C   powerful and effective
    D   clear and simple

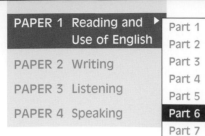
PAPER 1	Reading and ▸	Part 1
	Use of English	Part 2
PAPER 2	Writing	Part 3
		Part 4
PAPER 3	Listening	Part 5
PAPER 4	Speaking	**Part 6**
		Part 7

You are going to read an article about robot shops. Six sentences have been removed from the article. Choose from the sentences **A–G** the one which fits each gap (**37–42**). There is one extra sentence which you do not need to use.

Mark your answers **on the separate answer sheet**.

The robot shop

Like most ideas that seem absolutely revolutionary, the concept behind the robot shop is actually very simple. In fact, it has already been around for many years in the form of vending machines selling bars of chocolate or drinks. This idea has been further developed to create the first robot shop, which may eventually change the future of shopping.

The prototype robot shop in a suburb of London looks like a giant vending machine. **37** ☐ The display on the right is refrigerated and holds items such as milk, yoghurt and cheese, while the display on the left has an impressive selection of biscuits, coffee, cakes and crisps. It does not have the variety of conventional shops, but it can cope with a late-night request for bread or painkillers.

A central console is what allows you to actually do your shopping. You key in the code numbers of the goods you want, which are displayed just underneath each item in the window, and a huge robot arm reaches out and picks up each item, bringing it over to the console inside the shop.

An electronic display shows you the total you have to pay. **38** ☐ Unlike supermarkets, in robot shops you can only collect the goods after you've paid. When the robot arm finds the things you want, it drops them into a hatch and you reach inside to take them out. If this happened before you paid, you could easily walk off with the goods without having paid for them.

The system couldn't yet be described as entirely efficient. There's a lot of room for improvement. The robot arm represents one of the biggest problems. **39** ☐ The arm has to be very accurate in order to pick up the item it has reached for, carry it to the hatch and safely drop it into it.

The difficulty of judging customer attitudes is another reason why the robot shop has to be tested. Customers are still cautious about doing most of their shopping in a robot shop, but this is only to be expected; every new invention has been regarded with some suspicion at first. **40** ☐

The manufacturers of robot shops suggest that the small shopkeeper in inner-city areas represents their biggest potential client. **41** ☐ People in the area value the convenience of being able to pop out virtually all hours of the day and night for some item they have forgotten or suddenly feel like buying. Small shopkeepers are likely to invest in robot shop equipment, rather than employ part-time staff to work twenty-four hours a day.

The question is whether customers will prefer the impersonal service of a robot shop to the conventional type of shopping where there's human contact. **42** ☐ Machines do not take lunch breaks, they hardly ever make mistakes and they are never rude to customers. Isn't this the sort of efficiency people want from a shop these days?

A Not least of which are concerns about mechanical failure, especially when they occur in the middle of the night.

B The first thing you notice are the two large display windows which are absolutely packed with goods.

C The real question is whether, over the three-month testing period, enough people will overcome their doubts and start shopping here in significant numbers.

D For security reasons, you have to do this before the robot arm starts gathering your goods.

E Many shops like these only survive because they stay open late, or even around the clock in some cases.

F Experience with similar mechanised service equipment, such as cash dispensers, suggest that there are considerable advantages for both customers and shop owners.

G The challenge is to create a piece of machinery which will be delicate enough to pick up eggs but at the same time strong enough to pick up bottles of mineral water and baked-bean cans.

You are going to read part of an article in which four people talk about the sports lessons they had at school. For questions **43–52** choose from the people (**A–D**). The people may be chosen more than once.

Mark your answers **on the separate answer sheet**.

Which person

thinks sports encourage cooperation?	**43**
believes that experience of losing is important?	**44**
thinks one benefit of sports is learning to concentrate?	**45**
compares academic subjects to sports?	**46**
believes the Olympic spirit is essential today?	**47**
thinks sports help non-academic pupils?	**48**
thinks sports can teach objectivity and justice?	**49**
thinks schools should teach unusual sports?	**50**
thinks diet and health should be taught with sports?	**51**
thinks sports can make some children feel uncomfortable?	**52**

Sports at school

A Diane Townson

Looking back, I did enjoy sports lessons at school, even though I think most schools in those days assumed sports were basically for boys, and girls weren't encouraged to do well at sports. That attitude really annoys me, because the whole point of sports at school is to help kids develop the right attitudes, and it doesn't matter really how good you are. If you can't run as fast as an Olympic athlete, that doesn't matter – what matters is that you run as fast as you can. Schools are highly competitive environments and sports can teach children the importance of teamwork. To do well in almost everything else at school, like maths or history, you are rewarded for individual effort, but sports are about working together towards a common goal. Sports at school give children who are not high achievers a chance to excel at something.

B Colin Campbell

My own memories of sports lessons at school aren't particularly good, but that's mainly because of the type of school I went to. It was very unusual by British standards, with old-fashioned ways of teaching, and the headteacher didn't really think sports mattered at all. The school rarely organised sports events and never invested in sports equipment. There was very little emphasis on the importance of eating sensibly and the benefits of keeping fit and exercising properly. I believe that issues like obesity, anorexia, nutritional value of food, etc. should be included in sports lessons at school. Children should be encouraged to take part in competitive sports. Being competitive is part of human nature, and doing sports can provide an excellent outlet for this aggressiveness. Winning at sports can build up your self-esteem and confidence. On the other hand, since you can't expect to win every time, sports can also teach you how to be humble and realistic.

C Roger Dias

There are obvious benefits in having good sports classes at school. Children stay fit and learn the importance of fair play. Schools can introduce children to sports they would never otherwise have the opportunity of doing. For instance, I grew up in a big city, and we hardly ever travelled to the countryside as a family. At school we had a climbing wall in the gym, and we learnt rock climbing in sports class. When I moved to Europe, I took up rock climbing and was surprised by how good I was at it. Schools should offer a wide range of sports from the most popular ones, like football and basketball, to the less popular ones, like table tennis and climbing. Unfortunately, sports are often regarded as a sort of optional extra by certain schools and this is also reflected in the children's attitude to them.

D Helen Smith

The main point about sports is that they encourage peaceful competition. I think that's the basis of the Olympic spirit of Classical Greece, which nowadays is more important than ever before. Sports can teach you how to discipline yourself, how to remain focused on what you're doing and how to apply yourself to achieving a goal. I don't think sports are really about the sort of aggression and rage that you see sometimes in football matches, for instance. I certainly think teachers should discourage any form of aggression during sports classes. On top of that, we need to be more sensitive towards the feelings of children who are not fit or good at sports. Taking part in a sports lesson can be a major source of embarrassment and a traumatic experience for less athletic children.

You **must** answer this question. Write your answer in **140–190** words in an appropriate style.

1   In your English class you have been talking about free time. Now, your English teacher has asked you to write an essay.

Write an essay using **all** the notes and give reasons for your point of view.

> Some people say we all have too much free time and should spend more time studying or working. Do you agree?
>
> **Notes**
> Write about:
>
> 1. work or study hours
> 2. seeing family and friends
> 3. .... (your own idea)

Write an answer to **one** of the questions **2–5** in this part. Write your answer in **140–190** words in an appropriate style.

2   A new shop has recently opened in your area and your English teacher has asked you to write a review of it for the college English-language magazine. Describe the shop, what it sells and give your opinion of the staff in the shop. Would you recommend this shop to other people your age?

Write your **review**.

3   You see this announcement in an international magazine.

> **Do local traditions really matter?**
>
> As the world becomes smaller and globalisation has a greater effect on us all, is there any place for local traditions? Tell us about any traditions that you feel should be preserved.

Write your **article**.

4   (*for FIRST candidates only*)

You see this announcement on an English-language website.

> **Free photography course in New York!**
>
> Ten lucky people can attend a four-week photography course in New York for free, including accommodation and food!
>
> We are looking for people with an interest in photography, but beginners are welcome.
>
> Write to Mr Harvey Green, explaining why you should be offered a place.

Write your **letter of application**.

(*for FIRST FOR SCHOOLS candidates only*) You see this announcement on an English-language website.

> We are looking for stories from all over the world! Your story must begin with this sentence:
>
> *Dan knew he might regret answering the text message, but he did it anyway.*
>
> Your story must include:
> • a car
> • a present

Write your **story**.

5   (*for FIRST FOR SCHOOLS candidates only*) Answer the following question based on your reading of one of the set books.

Characters in books have to make important decisions. Write an **essay** about a decision that one of the characters had to make in the book or one of the short stories you have read. You should also say whether you would have made the same decision as the character.

PAPER 1 Reading and
         Use of English

PAPER 2 Writing

PAPER 3 Listening ▶ | Part 1 |
                        | Part 2 |
                        | Part 3 |
                        | Part 4 |

PAPER 4 Speaking

Track 29

You will hear people talking in eight different situations. For questions **1–8**, choose the best answer (**A**, **B** or **C**).

---

1 You hear a man talking to his friend about his choice of career.
   What does he say?
   A He wishes his current job was more exciting.
   B He has plans to change his profession.
   C He regrets not following his dream.

2 You hear a woman talking about being a student at university.
   Why did she study French?
   A because her parents wanted her to
   B because she had enjoyed her visit to the country
   C because she wanted to become a translator

3 You hear a man talking about acupressure.
   Which of the following does he say acupressure can do?
   A relieve headaches
   B change people's mood
   C prevent colds

4 You hear an actress talking about her new role.
   What character is she playing?
   A a bank manager
   B a mother
   C a taxi driver

5 You hear two students talking about remembering new vocabulary.
   What do they agree about?
   A The memorisation technique is boring.
   B The association technique is time-consuming.
   C The picture technique is effective.

6 You hear the captain of a plane talking to his passengers.
   Which city are they closest to at the moment?
   A Brussels
   B Rotterdam
   C Amsterdam

7 You hear a woman talking about taking up dancing as a hobby.
   How does she feel about it now?
   A surprised by the progress she's already made
   B very upset by her obvious lack of skill
   C motivated to improve her ability

8 You hear a man and a woman talking about an author's latest work.
   What does the woman think is a masterpiece?
   A the author's collection of short stories
   B the author's latest novel
   C the author's latest film script

🎧 **Track 30**

You will hear part of a careers talk by a nurse called Anne England. For questions **9–18**, complete the sentences with a word or short phrase.

Being a nurse

Anne was inspired to become a nurse when she heard her

        (9) .... talking about the job.

Anne's teachers told her she would need to improve her

        (10) .... a bit if she wanted to be a good nurse.

Anne hadn't expected to go to so many **(11)** .... when

        she was a student.

Anne's **(12)** .... helped her with some of her student

        projects.

Anne found learning how to **(13)** .... people safely was

        particularly useful.

When Anne got her first job, she had to go to work by

        (14) .... every day.

Anne didn't enjoy having to do a lot of **(15)** ....

People say Anne is much more **(16)** .... than she used

        to be.

One of Anne's patients gave her a **(17)** .... which she

        always wears.

If Anne wasn't a nurse, she would like to be an **(18)** ....

Track 31

You will hear five short extracts in which people are talking about a journal or magazine they read regularly. For questions **19–23**, choose from the list (**A–H**) what each speaker says. Use the letters only once. There are three extra letters which you do not need to use.

A The fashion photography is excellent.

B It provides an excellent news round-up.

Speaker 1 | 19 |

C It presents a variety of different views.

Speaker 2 | 20 |

D It features the best photographs.

Speaker 3 | 21 |

E It has good travel information.

Speaker 4 | 22 |

F It has information on things I buy.

Speaker 5 | 23 |

G It is both entertaining and informative.

H It has the most up-to-date information about fashion.

Track 32

You will hear a radio interview with a woman called Kay Stanley who is talking about a condition called dyslexia. For questions **24–30**, choose the best answer (**A**, **B** or **C**).

24   The Stanley Trust
     A   helped Kay a lot when she was a child.
     B   was started by Kay to help other people with dyslexia.
     C   was founded by Kay's father.

25   How did Kay's parents first realise she had dyslexia?
     A   She didn't know stories that other children could read.
     B   Her mother found her memorising audio books.
     C   She couldn't spell words that other children knew.

26   What was Kay told by an expert on dyslexia?
     A   She has a milder form of the condition.
     B   She will be able to overcome her problems by reading.
     C   Spelling will always be a particular problem for her.

27   How does dyslexia affect the way people think?
     A   It can make people think more creatively.
     B   It prevents them from solving problems effectively.
     C   It makes it harder for them to follow logic.

28   What made Kay work hard to improve her reading?
     A   It was the only way she could study acting.
     B   She didn't want people to think she was stupid.
     C   Her father encouraged her.

29   Kay feels that children with dyslexia should
     A   attend special schools.
     B   have special training to help them read.
     C   be treated like all other children at school.

30   How does Kay want to publicise the problem of dyslexia?
     A   by acting in a film about the subject
     B   by giving talks to parents of dyslexic children
     C   by setting a positive example

Part 1 (2 minutes)

The examiner (interlocutor) will ask each of you to speak briefly in turn and to give personal information about yourselves. You can expect a variety of questions, such as:

Do you enjoy going to the cinema or the theatre? (Why?)
Is the cinema in your town or district popular?
Was the last film you saw at the cinema or on television? What was it about?
What's your favourite TV programme? (Why?)

Part 2 (4 minutes)

You will each be asked to talk for a minute without interruption. You will each be given two different photographs in turn to talk about. After your partner has finished speaking, you will be asked a brief question connected with your partner's photographs.

1 Learning environments

Look at the two photographs on page 180 which show different learning environments.

Candidate A, compare these photographs, and say what you think about these two learning environments.

Candidate B, which of these learning environments would you prefer? (Why?)

2 Holidays

Look at the two photographs on page 181 which show different types of holiday.

Candidate B, compare these photographs, and say why you think the people have chosen these different types of holiday.

Candidate A, which of these two holidays would you prefer? (Why?)

Part 3 (4 minutes)

You will be asked to discuss something together without interruption by the examiner. You will have a page of ideas with a question to help you.

The shopping centre

Imagine your town is going to have a new shopping centre. Turn to page 182 which shows some ideas for how a new shopping centre could attract customers and a question for you to discuss. Talk to each other about how useful these ideas would be for attracting customers. Then decide which two ideas the shopping centre should have.

Part 4 (4 minutes)

The examiner will encourage you to develop the topic of your discussion in Part 3 by asking questions such as:

Do you prefer to shop alone or with friends?
Where do you like to go shopping? (Why?)
Do people in your country like shopping in small local shops? (Why? / Why not?)
What are the disadvantages of shopping in large shopping centres?
Are there any products that you can only find in large shopping centres?
Are there any special products sold in your town/city that would be impossible to buy in another country?

PAPER 1 Reading and Use of English

▶▶ PART 5

obstacle (n) something that makes it difficult to succeed

beat the odds (expr) to succeed even though there is little chance of doing so

dynamic (adj) active and energetic

non-profit-making organisation (n) an organisation whose aim is to help people, not to make money

smart (adj) clever

cockpit (n) the part of an aeroplane where the pilot sits

hooked (adj) wanting to do something all the time

scholarship (n) money given to a student to help pay for their studies

flight simulator (n) something that imitates the conditions inside an aircraft

take hold (expr) to begin to be important

donate (v) to give for no charge

component (n) a part

touch down (phr v) to land

fanfare (n) excitement and attention

boost (v) to increase

tackle (v) to deal with

from scratch (phr) without any previous knowledge

neuron (n) a type of brain cell

▶▶ PART 6

revolutionary (adj) completely different from what was done before

concept (n) an idea

prototype (n) an early example

conventional (adj) traditional and ordinary

console (n) central control panel

key in (v) to enter (numbers or information)

hatch (n) an opening

cautious (adj) taking care to avoid risks or danger

regard (v) to consider

suspicion (n) a doubt

potential (adj) possible

virtually (adv) almost

impersonal (adj) unemotional, lacking human contact

overcome (v) to deal with and control a problem

gather (v) to collect together

delicate (adj) gentle

▶▶ PART 7

attitude (n) a feeling about or toward someone or something

competitive (adj) involving or demanding competition, aggressive

individual (adj) working on your own

achiever (n) a person with a record of successes

excel (v) to do very well

equipment (n) useful items needed for a purpose (work, sports, etc.)

obesity (n) the condition of being too fat

anorexia (n) prolonged loss of appetite, resulting in low body weight

outlet (n) a release for emotions or energy

aggressive (adj) unfriendly, hostile, competitive

self-esteem (n) a sense of self-worth

fair play (expr) playing fairly and according to rules; not cheating

optional extra (phr) something additional that you can choose

reflect (v) to show or be a sign of a particular situation or feeling

discipline (v) to train to control the mind and body

sensitive (adj) understanding, aware

embarrassment (n) a feeling of shame, discomfort or self-consciousness

traumatic (adj) shocking, harmful

athletic (adj) having ability in sports

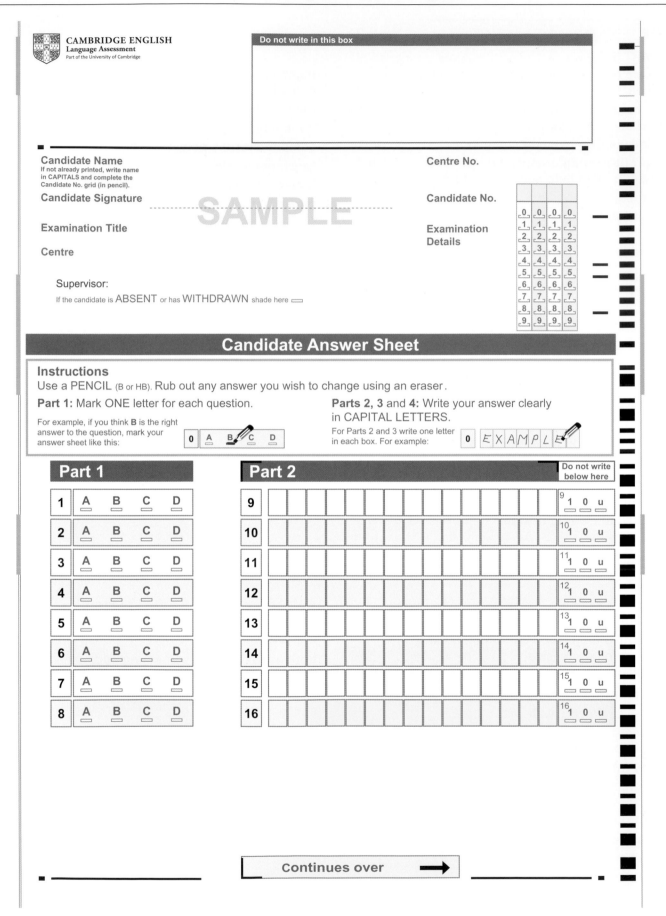

CAMBRIDGE ENGLISH
Language Assessment
Part of the University of Cambridge

Do not write in this box

Candidate Name
If not already printed, write name
in CAPITALS and complete the
Candidate No. grid (in pencil).

Candidate Signature

Examination Title

Centre

Supervisor:
If the candidate is ABSENT or has WITHDRAWN shade here ▭

SAMPLE

Centre No.

Candidate No.

Examination
Details

Candidate Answer Sheet

Instructions

Use a PENCIL (B or HB). Rub out any answer you wish to change using an eraser.

Part 1: Mark ONE letter for each question.

For example, if you think **B** is the right
answer to the question, mark your
answer sheet like this:

0 A B C D

Parts 2, 3 and **4:** Write your answer clearly
in CAPITAL LETTERS.

For Parts 2 and 3 write one letter
in each box. For example:

0 E X A M P L E

Part 1

1	A	B	C	D
2	A	B	C	D
3	A	B	C	D
4	A	B	C	D
5	A	B	C	D
6	A	B	C	D
7	A	B	C	D
8	A	B	C	D

Part 2

Do not write
below here

9
10
11
12
13
14
15
16

Continues over ➡

Part 6

	A	B	C	D	E	F	G
37	A	B	C	D	E	F	G
38	A	B	C	D	E	F	G
39	A	B	C	D	E	F	G
40	A	B	C	D	E	F	G
41	A	B	C	D	E	F	G
42	A	B	C	D	E	F	G

Part 7

	A	B	C	D
43	A	B	C	D
44	A	B	C	D
45	A	B	C	D
46	A	B	C	D
47	A	B	C	D
48	A	B	C	D
49	A	B	C	D
50	A	B	C	D
51	A	B	C	D
52	A	B	C	D

SAMPLE

Part 3 (Remember to write in CAPITAL LETTERS or numbers)

Do not write below here

17 1 0 u
18 1 0 u
19 1 0 u
20 1 0 u
21 1 0 u
22 1 0 u
23 1 0 u
24 1 0 u

Part 4 (Remember to write in CAPITAL LETTERS or numbers)

Do not write below here

25 2 1 0 u
26 2 1 0 u
27 2 1 0 u
28 2 1 0 u
29 2 1 0 u
30 2 1 0 u

SAMPLE

Part 5

	A	B	C	D
31	A	B	C	D
32	A	B	C	D
33	A	B	C	D
34	A	B	C	D
35	A	B	C	D
36	A	B	C	D

Continues over

Candidate Answer Sheet

CAMBRIDGE ENGLISH
Language Assessment
Part of the University of Cambridge

Do not write in this box

Candidate Name
If not already printed, write name in CAPITALS and complete the Candidate No. grid (in pencil).

Candidate Signature

Examination Title

Centre

SAMPLE

Centre No.

Candidate No.

Examination Details

Supervisor:
If the candidate is ABSENT or has WITHDRAWN shade here ▭

Test version: A B C D E F J K L M N   Special arrangements: S H

Instructions

Use a PENCIL (B or HB).
Rub out any answer you wish to change using an eraser.

Parts 1, 3 and 4:
Mark ONE letter for each question.

For example, if you think **B** is the right answer to the question, mark your answer sheet like this:

0 A ▭ B ▬ C ▭

Part 2:
Write your answer clearly in CAPITAL LETTERS.

Write one letter or number in each box.
If the answer has more than one word, leave one box empty between words.

For example:

0 N U M B E R 1 2

Turn this sheet over to start.

Part 1

	A	B	C
1	A	B	C
2	A	B	C
3	A	B	C
4	A	B	C
5	A	B	C
6	A	B	C
7	A	B	C
8	A	B	C

Part 2 (Remember to write in CAPITAL LETTERS or numbers)

SAMPLE

Do not write below here

9									9 1 0 u
10									10 1 0 u
11									11 1 0 u
12									12 1 0 u
13									13 1 0 u
14									14 1 0 u
15									15 1 0 u
16									16 1 0 u
17									17 1 0 u
18									18 1 0 u

Part 3

	A	B	C	D	E	F
19	A	B	C	D	E	F
20	A	B	C	D	E	F
21	A	B	C	D	E	F
22	A	B	C	D	E	F
23	A	B	C	D	E	F

Part 4

	A	B	C
24	A	B	C
25	A	B	C
26	A	B	C
27	A	B	C
28	A	B	C
29	A	B	C
30	A	B	C

TEST 1

▸▸ **PART 2**

Candidate A

Language bank

The first photograph might be a village in Asia, because of the style of the boats. People seem to be living in these boats.

On the other hand, the second photograph shows skyscrapers, probably with very expensive apartments for wealthy people. This could be a photo of any big, modern city.

Perhaps the people who live on the houseboats in the first photograph also work on the water. They might catch fish for a living, or use their boats to transport goods. This could be the reason why they have chosen to live on these boats.

I suppose the people who live in the skyscrapers want to be in the centre of the city. Maybe they work in the city and have chosen to live near their workplaces or they just prefer city life.

| Why have people chosen to live in these places? |

▸ 1

▸ 2

▶▶ **PART 2**

Candidate B

Language bank

The first photograph shows people in a very big theatre or opera house, and everyone is wearing formal clothes. It could be a classical music concert or opera.

In contrast, the people in the second photograph are younger, and it looks as if a concert is taking place outdoors. Unlike the people in the first photo, these people are casually dressed. This could be a pop or rock concert.

The people in the first photograph look quite serious, but they could be thinking about what they're going to see or hear when the performance starts. The second photograph shows people who are excited and seem to be enjoying themselves.

Both photos show people who like music, and are probably glad to be attending these performances.

How are the people feeling?

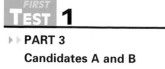

PART 3

Candidates A and B

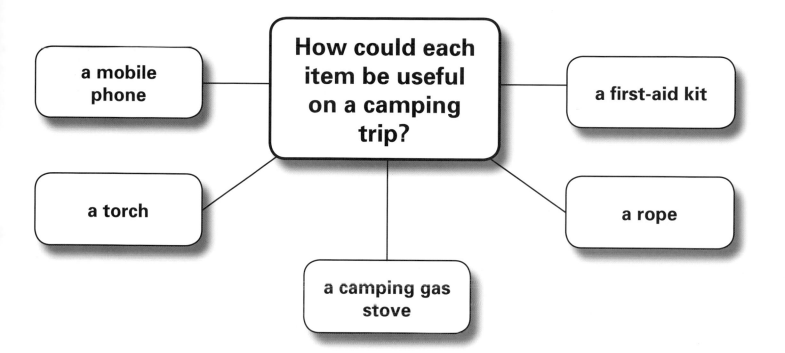

Language bank

A mobile phone would be useful for contacting friends or family, and if we had any problems, we would be able to phone for help. I agree, although we might not be able to use a mobile phone if we were in a remote place.

I think we would have to take a first-aid kit because someone could be hurt in an accident. But this might not be the most important thing to take.

If we had a torch, it would make it much easier to do lots of things, like putting up the tent in the dark, for example. I would agree with you about that.

Let's try to reach a decision. Are we agreed that we should take a torch? Unfortunately, I can't agree with you on that.

▶▶ **PART 2**

Candidate A

Language bank

Both these photos show people who seem to be working hard.

The young woman in the first photo is in a library, reading a book at a table; the young man behind her looks as if he's working hard too. The library is modern and light, and there are a lot of books on the shelves behind her.

Perhaps the woman has chosen to study in the library because she likes to work in a quiet place where other people are studying too. I imagine she can get any book she needs for her studies very easily in the library, so maybe she likes it for that reason as well.

The young man is in a busy café, working on his laptop. He looks as if he is concentrating hard, even though the people around him are talking. Maybe he's going to meet a friend there later, or maybe he prefers to work in a more relaxed atmosphere.

Personally, I prefer to study in quiet places, like at home or in a library. I find I work more efficiently if I'm not disturbed by other people making a noise.

| Why are the people working in these places? |

▶ 1

▶ 2

▸▸ **PART 2**

Candidate B

Language bank

The first photograph shows a small family consisting of a man and woman and a little girl who is probably their daughter. The parents are about thirty, and the girl is about ten years old. They seem happy and relaxed, and they're sitting on the grass, perhaps in a park.

The second photograph is more formal, as if a photographer asked the people to sit like this. There are three children sitting on the floor at the front, a girl aged about eight and two boys, probably her brothers, aged about five and twelve. There are four adults on the sofa behind them. Two of the adults are probably the parents of the children. And there is an older couple, probably the grandparents.

I suppose in a small family the child might get more attention from the parents, but the child could also be lonely. In a big family, with grandparents and several children, it could be harder to have some time to yourself, but you'd never be lonely, and you might grow up to be more sociable.

What would it feel like to grow up in these families?

▸ **1**

▸ **2**

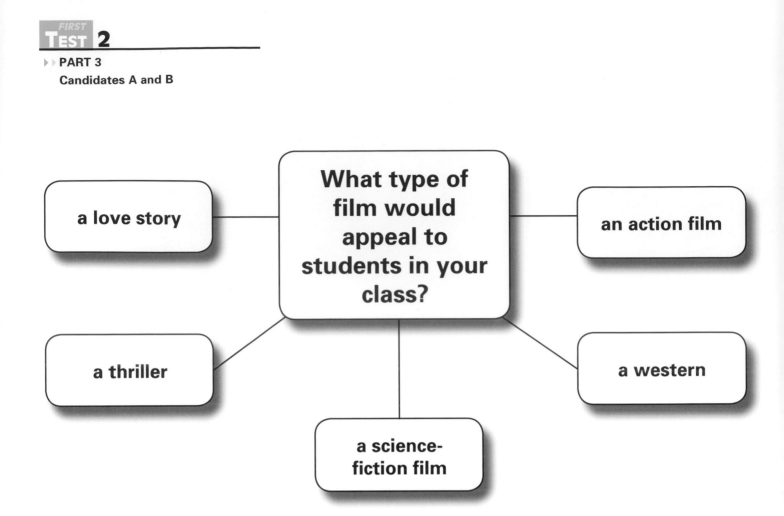

a love story

What type of film would appeal to students in your class?

an action film

a thriller

a western

a science-fiction film

Language bank

Who do you think would like that type of film? What sort of person would that type of film appeal to? Do you think the people in our class would prefer this type of film or that one?

I suggest we talk about each kind of film first. Let's decide who would like each of the films. Why don't we decide which kind of film we think would be most suitable? What about choosing the kind of film we like best?

I agree with you about a love story. I disagree that a thriller would be a good choice, because not everyone likes that sort of film. I don't think you're right about that. Do you agree that an action film would be popular? Don't you think we should choose a western?

▶▶ **PART 2**

Candidate A

Language bank

The first photograph shows a man in a shirt and tie sitting in what looks like a hotel restaurant or terrace. The hotel might be quite expensive. He looks as if he's drinking coffee, and there's fruit juice on the table, so he must be having breakfast. He's looking at something on his computer. Perhaps he's reading a work email.

In the second photograph some people are having a picnic. They're sitting on a rug or blanket on the grass. I think it's a mother and father and their two children, a boy and a girl. My impression is that they're having lunch.

I think the man in the first photo looks relaxed, while the people in the second photo look really happy and they're probably having fun.

Personally, I wouldn't like to stay in a posh hotel because I wouldn't feel relaxed. I enjoy being in the countryside, so I'd rather have a meal outdoors like the people in the second photograph.

> **How do the people feel in these situations?**

▶ 1

▶ 2

▸▸ **PART 2**

Candidate B

Language bank

In the first photograph a man is driving a sports car down a mountain road. The car seems to be coming towards the camera at high speed. It looks like a very expensive car.

The car in the second photograph is red and could be a vintage car. As in the first photo, a man is driving and looks as if he's enjoying himself. The car appears to be in excellent condition.

I think it would be exciting to drive both of these cars. I get the feeling that the car in the first photo is a lot faster than the one in the second photo. I often feel nervous if someone drives fast, but I like travelling by car. Being able to drive is important, and having a driving licence gives you a feeling of freedom and independence.

How would it feel to travel in these cars?

▸ 1

▸ 2

▶▶ **PART 3**
   Candidates A and B

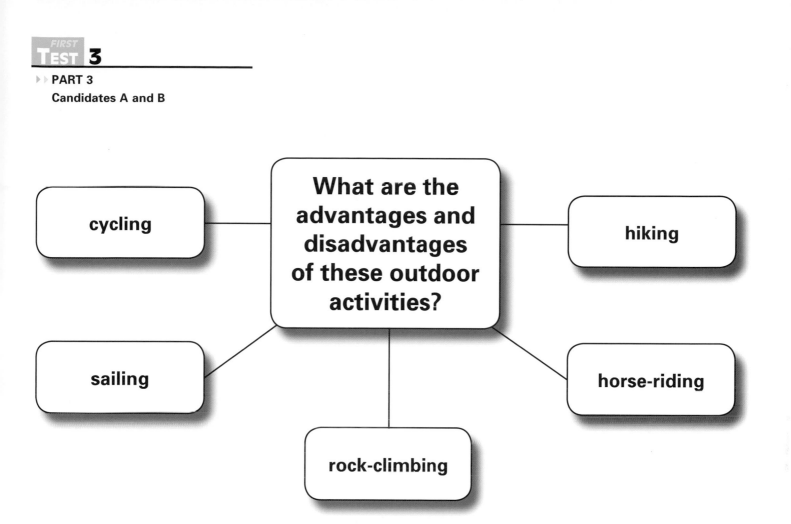

Language bank

What do you think are the advantages of this activity?
Do you think this activity would be suitable for young
teenagers? Does this activity have any disadvantages
in this situation?

I'd say rock-climbing is exciting, but it might take
a long time to learn to do properly. On the one
hand, hiking can be very satisfying, but some of
the teenagers might find it terribly boring. I think
teenagers would love sailing, which is very good fun
and less dangerous than climbing.

If we have to choose two of these activities, I'd
suggest sailing and cycling. Would you agree with me
on that? Don't you think young people would learn a
lot from these activities? I think they would, too.

It seems that we don't agree on this, because you
believe climbing would be a suitable choice here, and I
don't share that view.

▶▶ **PART 2**

Candidate A

Language bank

Both photos show different working environments.

There is a woman working at a desk with a pile of papers and files next to the computer. She's concentrating hard. She could be an accountant or a lawyer.

The woman might be thinking about all the work she has to do. I would imagine that she must be feeling overworked and stressed.

The man in the second photo is standing in a building or wooden structure, hammering a nail into some wood. I would guess that the man is helping to build this. He is wearing casual working clothes and a hat to protect his head.

This man must be quite fit, and perhaps he enjoys working with his hands. He is concentrating on his work and seems to be making sure he is doing everything properly.

How are the people feeling in these different situations?

▶ **1**

▶ **2**

▶▶ **PART 2**

Candidate B

Language bank

Both photos show leisure activities.

The boy in the first photo is balancing on a skateboard with one arm up in the air, and it looks as though he might have just jumped off a wall on his skateboard. You would have to be fit and active to enjoy this, and I think the sort of person who would go skateboarding would love adventure and taking risks in life.

The woman in the second photo looks relaxed. She is sitting on a sofa, reading a book. It looks as though she is concentrating on what she is reading, so I'd say the book is probably very interesting. Someone who likes reading would enjoy this activity, or perhaps someone who has been working hard and deserves a rest.

Reading is a more passive activity compared to skateboarding.

| What sort of person would enjoy each of these activities? |

▶ **1**

▶ **2**

▶▶ **PART 3**

  Candidates A and B

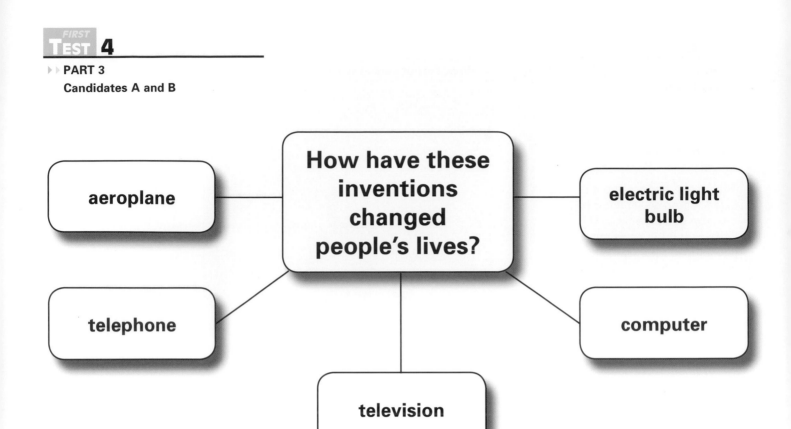

Language bank

Let's think about how important these inventions have been to us. Which ones have changed people's lives, would you say?

If the electric light bulb hadn't been invented, our lives today would be very different. Do you agree with me on that?

It's hard to imagine life without some of these inventions, like the telephone. On the other hand, air travel has made the world smaller and changed many people's lives.

If we think of inventions we could not do without today, I'd say the computer is the most important.

You're right about that. However, in terms of changing people's lives, I'd say the electric light bulb is the most important.

I agree to a certain extent. But I also think that television has improved the quality of our life.'

Shall we make a decision?

▶▶ **PART 2**

Candidate A

Language bank

I get the impression that this type of train is very modern and fast, so perhaps it's designed for public transport in a big city or between cities. It would seem to me that people who are in a hurry and have no time to waste would choose to travel by train.

The bus looks very crowded and the people look quite bored or fed up. Perhaps the people who are standing up would prefer to have a seat. I imagine this is a local city bus, because it doesn't look very luxurious. The passengers are probably travelling a short distance.

They might have chosen to travel by bus because it's cheaper or because they really had no other choice.

Why do people use these different means of transport?

▸▸ **PART 2**

Candidate B

Language bank

The man and woman in the first photograph look very happy and are both laughing. They are wearing very formal clothes and look very smart.

I assume these people have dressed formally to go to a wedding reception, celebrate an anniversary or have dinner in a posh restaurant.

The man and woman in the second photo are younger and are wearing casual clothes that would not be suitable for a formal celebration.

The people look relaxed and happy, and their clothes look comfortable and suitable for the weather. It looks as though they are out riding their bikes, and they would need to wear this type of clothing for the activity.

> **Why have the people chosen to wear these sorts of clothes?**

▸ 1

▸ 2

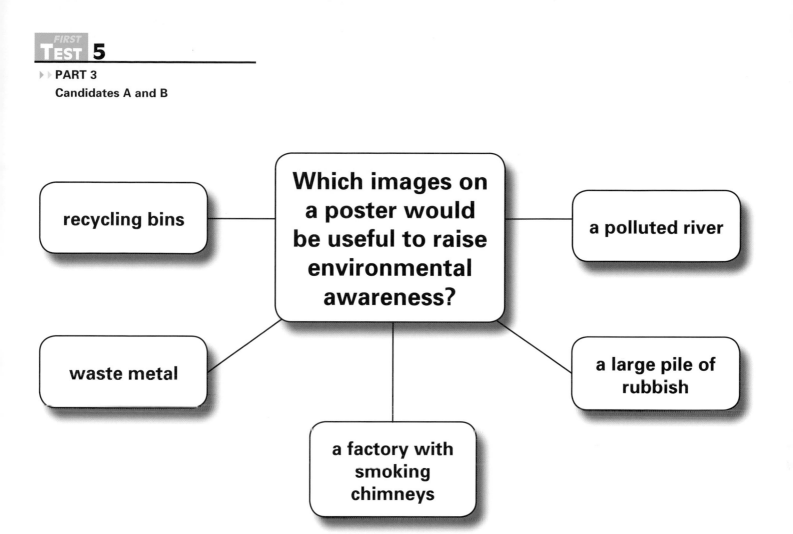

Which images on a poster would be useful to raise environmental awareness?

- recycling bins
- a polluted river
- waste metal
- a large pile of rubbish
- a factory with smoking chimneys

Language bank

Would you like to start?

The poster should illustrate ways of dealing with pollution. Don't you agree?

I would prefer a photo that illustrates the problems that pollution can cause to the environment. Do you see my point?

If I had to choose between a photo of a factory with smoking chimneys and one of waste metal, I would definitely go for the first one.

I'm afraid I disagree. Don't you think a photo of recycling bins would be more effective?

We haven't talked about this one. What do you think of it?

Perhaps you're right. I think we should make a decision now, so shall we choose the factory and the recycling bins?

▶▶ **PART 2**

Candidate A

Language bank

In the first photograph the artist appears to be painting the scene around him. I think an artist should paint a picture that is true to life. In my view, a picture should reflect the real world around us.

I would like to have this painting because it shows a peaceful landscape. I like the relaxed and tranquil mood of the first painting.

The artist in the second photograph is also facing slightly away from us, working on her painting. The photograph may have been taken inside the artist's studio, or she could be painting a wall in a school, for example, or even outdoors.

The painting in the second photo has a lot of faces, which look quite childish. People who appreciate modern, more abstract ways of expression would probably prefer this painting to the first one.

Which painting do you like most and why?

Language bank

The two women in the first photo seem to be choosing fruit or vegetables from a stall. One of them has a basket in her hand. It isn't clear whether this is a market stall or a stall outside a greengrocer's shop.

If you shop like this, you can select the things you want and check them carefully, which is an advantage. I imagine things are often cheaper in a market, too. Some customers might enjoy the friendly, personal atmosphere of shopping in a market or at a local greengrocer's.

The second photograph shows part of a supermarket, with a lot of vegetables on display. Some of the vegetables are loose, and others are in plastic packaging.

Supermarkets have a very wide variety of goods of different brands. Some things, such as clothes, may be cheaper in supermarkets. It is more convenient to go to a supermarket and do all your shopping in one place, especially for families who perhaps go shopping once a week. On the other hand, supermarkets can be very impersonal.

What are the advantages of shopping in each place?

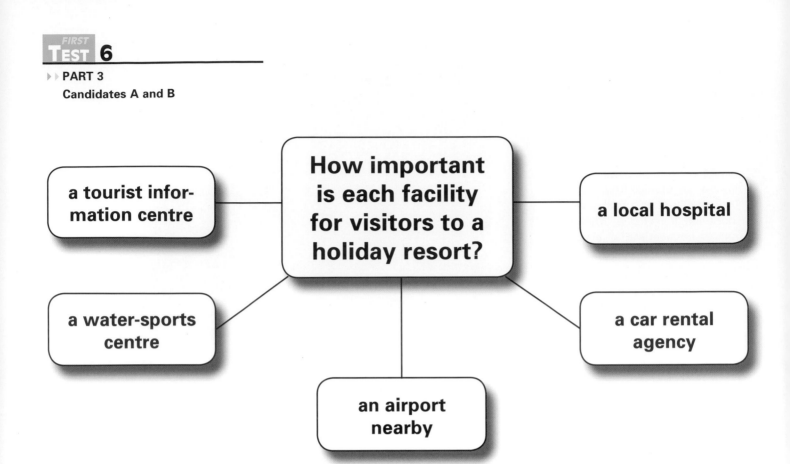

a tourist information centre

How important is each facility for visitors to a holiday resort?

a local hospital

a water-sports centre

a car rental agency

an airport nearby

Language bank

The point I'd like to make is that the majority of visitors would appreciate an airport nearby more than any other facility.

I don't completely agree with you. A lot of people these days want to visit places while on holiday, so a car rental agency would be a good idea.

That may be true, but I'd say most holidaymakers like to know medical care is available if necessary, so having a small hospital in the resort would be essential.

I think that the hospital should be the number one priority. Now, let's discuss what other facility the resort should have. What about a tourist information centre?

That's a very good point; a tourist information centre can help you organise your holiday, plan visits and sightseeing tours, but is this more important than a water sports centre, for example?

I consider the tourist information centre essential, so perhaps we have different views on this.

Well, we'll just have to agree to disagree!

▸▸ **PART 2**

Candidate A

Language bank

The young man in the first photo is holding a sports trophy, so he must have won a competition or have been in the winning team. Judging by his clothes, I'd say he is probably a basketball player.

In the background I imagine that there are a lot of spectators; this is probably an important sporting event, so the man must feel very proud of himself and pleased with his achievement. He must be feeling both exhausted after training and practising hard and relieved that the game or competition is over.

The young man and woman in the second photo are holding a small baby; it looks as though the baby is only a few weeks old, and they may still be learning how to look after him or her.

I'm sure the parents will never forget the day their baby was born. Both parents are smiling at the baby, and there can be no doubt that they are absolutely delighted to have a son or daughter.

> **What makes these moments special for these people?**

▸ 1

▸ 2

> > **PART 2**
> > **Candidate B**

Language bank

The first photo shows people in a desert. There are some large tents in the desert. We can see the desert stretching out into the distance. There are quite a few people here, wearing long robes and with their heads covered. There are also several camels walking along.

It must be very hot here, although I suppose people who are born here become accustomed to the heat. I don't think I could get used to living in such a hot climate. I expect it would be very dry and dusty as well as hot.

The house in the second photograph has a thatched roof. It looks old-fashioned and picturesque. Behind the house there are some trees, and there are more hills in the background. The sky is blue with some clouds, but I think the sun is shining.

The green grass and trees suggest the climate is quite wet, which might make life a bit uncomfortable. I think I would prefer this climate to the desert climate in the first photo.

What would it be like to live in each of these climates?

▶ **1**

▶ **2**

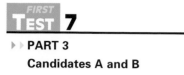

▶▶ **PART 3**
Candidates A and B

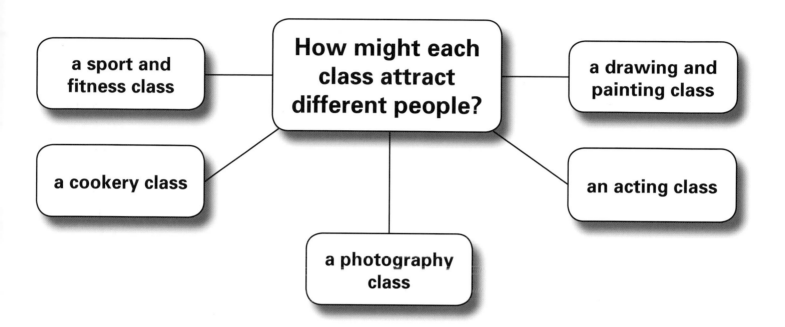

a sport and fitness class

a cookery class

How might each class attract different people?

a drawing and painting class

an acting class

a photography class

Language bank

I suppose sport and fitness classes would appeal to a lot of different people, of all ages. Perhaps the college should make these classes a priority.

I disagree; I think cookery classes would be more popular with people in a small town.

I see your point, but on the other hand, people learn to cook in their families; photography classes would be more entertaining and enjoyable.

What's your view on acting classes? Don't you agree that they would mainly attract younger people?

Since we have to choose two classes, can we agree that one of them should be a hobby and the other should be something useful, like the cookery class?

That sounds reasonable. In that case let's say one class should be cookery. We've got four options left. Which one should be our second choice?

▶▶ **PART 2**

Candidate A

Language bank

The teenagers in the first photo are sitting in a classroom writing something. They seem to be concentrating hard. They are all sitting in a row, and there are probably other students doing the same thing in front of them. There is a board behind them with some writing on it, and there's probably a teacher in the classroom with them. People can learn a lot in a classroom environment, especially if all the students are focusing quietly on their work.

The second photograph shows a group of younger children standing in front of a pile of plastic bottles. The man could be their teacher, and he must be talking to them about the benefits of recycling.

This is a more relaxed learning environment, and the children look motivated and interested in the subject. It seems to be quite a small group of children, so I suppose a pupil would get more attention from the teachers at this school.

What do you think about these two learning environments?

▶ 1

▶ 2

▸▸ **PART 2**

Candidate B

Language bank

The first photograph shows a group of people in the desert, with the Sphinx in the background, so this must be Egypt. It looks as though the people are tourists and one of the people at the front might be a guide explaining the history of the pyramids.

A tour like this might be a cheaper and easier way to see some interesting historical sights, because you would have an expert guide to explain everything.

It could be that these people have chosen to have a holiday in a group because they are members of a club or society, perhaps people with a common interest, or they may just be on a guided tour organised at the site.

The second photograph shows a man relaxing by a lake, with a pile of books next to him. He is looking at a laptop computer. This type of holiday would be more relaxing than the type of holiday shown in the first photo.

It would probably appeal to people who want to stay in a beautiful place and have a quiet time and who may not be particularly interested in going sightseeing or visiting tourist attractions.

Why have the people chosen these different types of holiday?

▸ 1

▸ 2

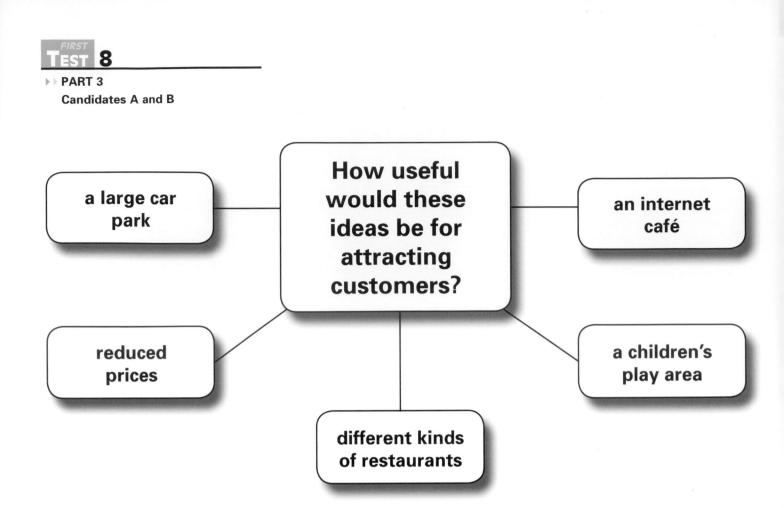

Language bank

Why don't we start by looking at the ideas?

My first choice would be the children's play area. I think that most families go shopping with their children, and having a place to leave them would be a good way to attract customers.

I couldn't agree more, but perhaps we're overlooking a very simple point: customers want to save money when they go shopping, so shops that have sales and reduced prices would be very popular.

Obviously, that is an important point, but what about the idea of having different kinds of restaurants? Don't you feel that would attract customers?

As we have to choose two of these ideas, I suggest choosing the car park and the reduced prices.

Preparing, planning and checking

▶▶ Preparing for the Writing Paper

One of the best ways to improve your writing skills is to read as widely as possible. This will help you to expand your range of vocabulary and grammatical structures. You also need to study the basic text types which you may be asked to produce in the exam, and have a good understanding of their basic features: layout, organisation, style and register (level of formality). You should also practise completing writing tasks in the time allowed in the exam. Remember the criteria the examiners will use in awarding marks:

- Has the candidate achieved the purpose stated in the instructions?
- Does the text have a positive general effect on the target reader?
- Does the text cover all the content points?
- Is the text well organised and are ideas linked appropriately?
- Has language been used accurately?
- Does the text show a good range of vocabulary and grammatical structures?
- Is the register appropriate for the task?
- Is the layout appropriate?

If possible, ask an experienced teacher to provide feedback on pieces of writing you produce when you are practising for the exam. This will help you to learn what kind of mistakes you frequently make so that you can avoid them. For example, if you often make mistakes with a certain tense, you can ask your teacher to explain it to you again, or you can use a good grammar guide to help you. It's also a good idea to make a list of expressions that you can include in your exam text, such as the useful phrases you find with the model answers in this section.

▶▶ Planning your answer

The most useful lesson to learn about writing is the importance of planning what to write before you actually start writing. In the exam you will only have time to write your text once, so you should make time to write a plan before you begin writing. This will help you to write your exam text more easily.

Always read the question carefully and make sure you understand the following:

- Who are you writing for (a friend, a teacher, other students)?
- What are the points you must include in your answer?

- Does the text type (an email, an article, a report, a review) have any particular layout requirements?
- Do you have the necessary vocabulary to answer the question on the topic?

When you are sure you understand what you have to do to answer the exam task, prepare a plan of what you are going to write. It doesn't matter if you change your plan or cross things out – nobody will read it. But it has to show clearly the different sections of your writing and which points you must include in which section (i.e. in the introduction, main body, and conclusion). When you look at the plan carefully, you might want to change it; for example, one point might be better in a different paragraph, or you might realise you will be repeating yourself. When you are satisfied with your plan, you will find it much quicker to write your text. Give yourself five minutes to make your plan before you start writing.

▶▶ Question 5, the set text task (*FIRST FOR SCHOOLS only*)

If you choose to write about one of the set texts, remember that the question may ask for an essay, article, email or letter. You may be asked to write about the characters, relationships or themes in the book. Make sure you know the story well, as you will need to support your views with examples from the book. When answering the question, think carefully about the target reader, and plan your answer accordingly.

Remember: Do **NOT** answer the set text question if you have not read the book.

▶▶ Checking

Most people make more mistakes than usual when they are writing under exam conditions. Always give yourself at least five minutes at the end to read through your work. First, check that you have answered the question correctly and that you have included all the information that was required. Second, check for mistakes in grammar, spelling, punctuation, etc. You should have enough writing experience by now to know where you often make mistakes – spelling certain words, for example, or using a particular type of punctuation.

If you need to change something in your text, make the correction carefully and make sure it is still easy for the examiner to read your work. If you need to cross out something you have written, just put one line through the word or words.

1 Essay

▶▶ Exam task – Part 1

You **must** answer this question. Write your answer in **140–190** words in an appropriate style.

In your English class you have been talking about the internet. Now, your English teacher has asked you to write an essay.

Write an essay using **all** the notes and give reasons for your point of view.

Do you think the internet has a negative effect on people's lives?

Notes

Write about:

1. communicating with friends
2. news and current affairs
3. .... (your own idea)

Useful phrases

Introducing the topic

To begin with ...

The first point I would like to make is ...

As some of us know, / As we all know, ...

Most people believe ...

Expressing opinions

It seems / appears to me that ...

I agree / disagree with ...

I am in favour of / I am against ...

For me, the most important ... is ...

Discussing pros and cons

On the one hand, ... / On the other hand, ...

However, ...

Nevertheless, ...

There are many arguments against / in favour of ...

Giving examples

For example / instance, ...

One example of ... is ...

... such as ...

Conclusion

To sum up, I believe there are advantages ...

In conclusion, ...

On balance, ...

▶▶ Approach

▶ Make sure your writing is well organised and clearly paragraphed, starting with an introduction and ending with a conclusion summarising your opinion.

▶ You need to write about the two elements in the notes, as well as adding an idea of your own. This third idea must be different from the other two, and cannot simply be your conclusion at the end of the essay. Think about what your own idea will be before you start writing. Read the question carefully and write a brief plan so you know what to include in each paragraph.

▶ The register should be neutral or semi-formal, and even if you have strong opinions on the topic, you should try to express them in an objective way and look at both sides of the argument.

State the general topic in the first paragraph.

The use of the internet is now widespread. It is part of most people's lives, and some believe that its overall effects are harmful to society.

One way of writing this kind of essay is to present the advantages of the statement or situation in one paragraph. Use the two points in the notes and add one of your own (here, the third point is about using the internet to help with homework).

As we all know, the internet makes it easy to keep in touch with friends or family, for example by using social networking sites. You can also find out about events in the wider world almost as soon as they have happened. Moreover, students use the internet to find useful information for homework and college projects.

You can present the disadvantages of the statement or situation in a separate paragraph.

On the other hand, there are disadvantages too. For example, people can spend so much time chatting to friends on their computers that they rarely meet them face-to-face. Furthermore, the news that people see on the internet is not always accurate. Accuracy can also be a problem for students using the internet for their homework; unless it is from a reliable website, it may be incorrect.

Use linking words or expressions to list the main points (advantages or disadvantages) in your paragraph.

Sum up the main points and say whether there are more advantages than disadvantages. Show clearly whether you agree, disagree or partly agree with the statement.

On balance, I think there are more advantages than disadvantages to using the internet. As long as people are careful and do not automatically believe everything they see on it, then the internet can be a positive part of their lives.

2 Email

▶▶ **Exam task – Part 2**

You have received this email from your English-speaking friend, Adam.

> **From:** Adam
>
> **Subject:** Exchange programme
>
> I've been offered the opportunity to come to your town on an exchange student programme. How easy is it to find accommodation? What is the transport like? And what is life like in your area? Do you think I should take up the offer?
>
> Write soon!
>
> Adam

Write your **email.**

Useful phrases

Introduction
Thanks for your message / email.
Sorry I haven't written before.
I'm really glad / sorry / pleased
  to hear …

Body of email
In my view / opinion, …
It would be a good idea to …
You should / shouldn't …
Don't forget to …
If I were you, I would / I'd …

Conclusion
Well, that's all for now.
I hope this is helpful.
Do keep in touch.
Write soon.
Look after yourself.
Give my love / regards to …

▶▶ **Model answer**

Dear Adam,

In the introduction greet your friend.

I was really pleased to get your email last week and to hear that you might be coming on an exchange programme. Sorry I haven't written back before now, but I've been very busy working in my parents' shop.

In your email you asked me about accommodation. There is a student residence not far from our apartment; I can find out if you could get a room there, and how much it will cost.

Divide your email into short paragraphs. Make sure each paragraph is on a different topic.

The bus service here is very efficient and reliable. The college is within walking distance from the town centre, and it would take you about 20 minutes to walk there.

The exam question requires you to give information about your area and advice about the exchange programme.

I think the exchange programme is a wonderful opportunity for you to spend time away from New York. Life here is very relaxing, the pace of life is slow, and the people are friendly. If I were you, I wouldn't think twice!

I'm really looking forward to seeing you here and showing you around my favourite places. Do write and tell me what you decide.

Finish your email in an informal way. Send greetings and ask the reader to write back.

Look after yourself,

Mike

3 Review

▶▶ **Exam task – Part 2**

You see this announcement in your college English-language magazine.

> ### Everyone has a favourite film.
>
> What makes a certain film mean so much to us?
>
> Write a review of your favourite film, and tell us why you like it so much.
> If we publish your review, you will win free film tickets for two people.

Write your **review**.

Useful phrases

Adjectives
exciting, amusing, gripping, absorbing, excellent, outstanding, hilarious, fascinating

Adverbs
extremely, incredibly, awfully, terribly, amazingly, surprisingly, particularly

Film-related vocabulary
The story is set …
The main characters …
It is produced / directed by …
The performance is …
The pace is slow / fast …
The message conveyed is …
The special effects are …
low-budget film, script, audiences, blockbuster

▶▶ **Model answer**

A review is a piece of writing where you are asked to give your opinion about a TV programme, a film or play you have watched.

Decide how formal the language should be; if you are writing for a magazine, the language can be quite informal.

Provide a brief summary of the plot and comment on the main characters.

List the things that you liked most about the film.

Film review: **Titanic**

My favourite film is Titanic, a wonderful story with incredible special effects. Titanic is not only a commercial success but also a good film.

In this film a rich young woman on the luxurious Titanic meets a struggling artist and they fall helplessly in love. When the ship sinks, he saves her life but drowns. The young woman never forgets him or stops loving his memory. The two main characters are fascinating and they have a wonderful on-screen chemistry.

The film is very realistic and the scenes when the ship is sinking are extremely dramatic. You can feel the panic of the people trying to get away, and this part of the film is particularly gripping! Although the film's success is partly based on its amazing special effects and action sequences, the director also focuses on how characters act in the crisis, which makes it an emotional film to watch.

The sinking of the Titanic may be one of the most important lessons for humanity. The great ship was thought to be unsinkable. People thought they had conquered nature. Its maiden voyage proved how wrong they were.

Make the introduction interesting without giving details about the film.

Try to make the review interesting by using dramatic and sophisticated language. Avoid repeating simple adjectives like *good*, or *bad*. Use adjectives like *fascinating*, *gripping* or *dramatic* to describe people or things.

The conclusion should summarise what you have said in the review or focus on the main message of the film.

4 Article

▶▶ Exam task – Part 2

You have seen this announcement in an English-language magazine.

> **We want your articles!**
> ### Giving gifts
> What's the most thoughtful gift you've ever received? Why do you think giving gifts is important? Do you think the best gifts are the most expensive ones?
>
> We'll publish the best articles in our magazine next month.

Write your **article**.

Useful phrases

Ordering language
First of all, …
Secondly, / Next, …
Another point is …
Finally …

Involving the reader
Have you ever …?
Can you imagine …?
I think you will agree that …
What would you do if …?

Giving your opinion
It seems to me that …
In my opinion …
To my mind …
As far as I'm concerned …
(Personally), I think / believe that …

▶▶ Model answer

An article is a piece of writing on a particular topic for a newspaper, magazine, newsletter, website or other publication.

Use neutral language for your article (not too formal or informal). You can address the reader personally by using 'you'.

Make your article lively and entertaining. Use descriptive language.

Conclude your article with a summary of what you have said, and give your opinion if appropriate.

Have you ever received a really thoughtful gift? The best gift I've ever been given was a picture from my ten-year-old niece, which she had drawn for my birthday. It wasn't an expensive gift, but it was one of the most thoughtful I've ever received. The picture was decorated with hand-drawn images of the things I love best: flowers, ice cream and birds.

Personally, I think it's important to give gifts to show you care about the people in your life. The picture my niece made was so nice because it demonstrated that she understands the things that make me happy. As far as I'm concerned, you don't have to spend a fortune on a gift: something home-made and personal is just as lovely to receive as a diamond ring or a fast car. And you don't need to wait for a special occasion such as a birthday; you can give gifts any day of the year to show someone you love them.

Remember, it isn't how much you spend on a gift that matters, but the thought you put into giving something you think the other person will enjoy.

Gain the reader's interest in the title and introduction, for example, ask a question to attract the reader's attention.

An article expresses your personal point of view and it does not need to be objective.

5 Report (for FIRST candidates only)

▶▶ **Exam task – Part 2**

Your local tourist office is preparing a brochure for tourists. Write a report suggesting a local tradition that you think should be included in the brochure. Include details about the tradition, such as what it means to local people, and what people do to celebrate the tradition.

Write your **report**.

Useful phrases

Introduction
This report is intended / designed to ...
The purpose of this report is to ...
The aim of this report is to ...

Making suggestions / recommendations
I would recommend ...
I suggest that ...

Conclusion
In conclusion, ...
In my view, / opinion, ...

▶▶ **Model answer**

You can use paragraph headings, numbering or bullet points to organise the information in a clear way.

The purpose of this report is to suggest a tradition which could be included in the brochure which might be of interest to visitors to our region. I would recommend including the tradition of Bonfire Night in the UK.

State the aim of the report in the introduction.

What is Bonfire Night?

Bonfire Night is a British celebration which takes place on 5th November each year. Originally, the tradition celebrated a historical event, although nowadays it is a social occasion.

What happens on Bonfire Night?

Bonfire Night is celebrated in the autumn, when it goes dark early in the evening. Fireworks are lit and big fires are made. In many towns, public firework displays are organised, and bonfire parties are held in people's gardens. Special food is eaten, too, such as toffee apples or jacket potatoes.

The language should be formal and impersonal (e.g. passive forms).

What does Bonfire Night mean to people?

Bonfire Night celebrations bring friends and families together in order to share a night of fun and a sense of community.

In the conclusion you should give your opinion and/or make a recommendation, depending on the wording of the exam question.

Conclusion

In conclusion, I suggest that the brochure for tourists should also include photographs relating to Bonfire Night. In my view, the local tradition mentioned in this report would appeal to visitors.

Don't write your name at the end of the report.

6 Letter of application (*for FIRST candidates only*)

▶▶ **Exam task – Part 2**

You see this advertisement in your college English-language magazine.

Summer jobs!

Could you be a guide for visitors to your area?

Excellent pay for part-time job guiding English-speaking visitors.

You must be available to work evenings and weekends.

Write your letter of application to the manager of *Visitors Unlimited*, Mr Sadler.

Write your **letter of application**.

Useful phrases

Introduction

I have seen your advertisement in our local newspaper …

I am writing in connection with the job vacancy you have advertised …

I am writing about …

I am writing to apply for …

Body of letter

I am … years old and I …

I have a good command of …

I have a good knowledge of …

I have worked …

I would be suitable for the job …

Conclusion

I would welcome the opportunity to …

I look forward to hearing from you / to your reply.

▶▶ **Model answer**

In a formal letter start with Dear *Mr / Mrs* …

Dear Mr Sadler,

I am writing in connection with the job vacancy you have advertised for a guide for visitors to this region.

In the introduction say briefly why you are writing.

Give information about yourself if you are writing to apply for a job.

I am 19 years old and have just finished my first year at university, studying Economics. I would be available to work from the beginning of June until the end of August, including evenings and weekends. I lived in London for a year when I was younger, and I am fluent in English. I am an outgoing person with a good sense of humour, and I am confident I would get on with visitors to this region.

Express the information in the exam question in your own words. Don't copy directly from the question.

Make sure you include all the necessary information given in the exam question.

I have travelled extensively in this part of the country, and I am familiar with several places that would be of interest to visitors. For example, the Folk Museum in the centre of town has fascinating exhibitions, the cathedral is popular with sightseers, and the old town has some interesting traditional restaurants.

I would welcome the opportunity of meeting you in person to discuss this. I look forward to your reply.

Finish by saying that you look forward to hearing from the other person.

If you know the person's name, end with *Yours sincerely*. If not, end with *Yours faithfully*.

Yours sincerely,
Maria Barone

7 Story (for FIRST FOR SCHOOLS candidates only)

▶▶ **Exam task – Part 2**

You have seen this announcement in an international English-language magazine for teenagers.

Stories wanted

We are looking for stories for our magazine for teenagers. Your story must begin with this sentence:

There was no moon that night, and we were not expecting a storm.

Your story must include:
- a boat
- a mobile phone.

Write your **story**.

Useful phrases

Setting the scene
There were three of us …
My family had rented a cottage …
It was a cold winter night …
I had never been to …

Sequencing events
At the beginning …
As soon as …
First …
Then …
Afterwards …
Finally …
In the end …

Reaction to events
I was petrified …
I was numb with fear …
I was shocked …
I stood there speechless …
I was so embarrassed …

▶▶ **Model answer**

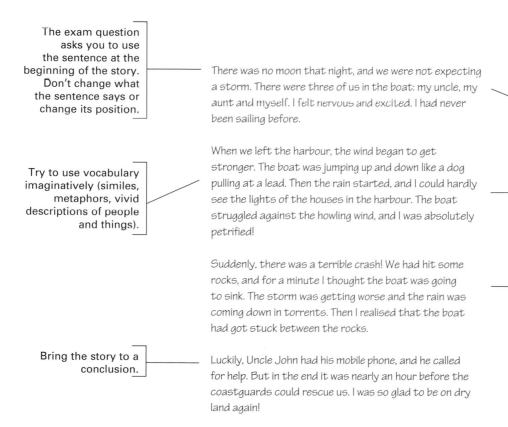

The exam question asks you to use the sentence at the beginning of the story. Don't change what the sentence says or change its position.

There was no moon that night, and we were not expecting a storm. There were three of us in the boat: my uncle, my aunt and myself. I felt nervous and excited. I had never been sailing before.

Begin the story in an interesting way. Set the scene: explain who the narrator is, say when and where the story takes place.

When we left the harbour, the wind began to get stronger. The boat was jumping up and down like a dog pulling at a lead. Then the rain started, and I could hardly see the lights of the houses in the harbour. The boat struggled against the howling wind, and I was absolutely petrified!

Try to use vocabulary imaginatively (similes, metaphors, vivid descriptions of people and things).

Describe the events and people's feelings and reactions to them.

Suddenly, there was a terrible crash! We had hit some rocks, and for a minute I thought the boat was going to sink. The storm was getting worse and the rain was coming down in torrents. Then I realised that the boat had got stuck between the rocks.

Present the main events of the story in chronological order. Use narrative tenses (past simple, past continuous, past perfect, etc.) and linking words (*when, by the time, within seconds,* etc.) to sequence events.

Bring the story to a conclusion.

Luckily, Uncle John had his mobile phone, and he called for help. But in the end it was nearly an hour before the coastguards could rescue us. I was so glad to be on dry land again!

Introduction to the DVD-ROM

This edition of *Exam Essentials* Practice Tests for students of Cambridge English: First (FCE) includes a brand new DVD-ROM which focuses on the Speaking test component of the Cambridge English: First examination. The DVD-ROM includes two videos:

• a complete Cambridge English: First Speaking test based on Test 3 of the Practice tests.
• a short clip giving valuable advice about the Cambridge English: First Speaking test.

To maximise learning from the complete Cambridge English: First Speaking test, the following PDFs are also available on the DVD-ROM:

• a worksheet for individual or class use
• an answer key for the worksheet
• the complete script of the Speaking test.

A complete Speaking test

A full Cambridge English: First Speaking test interview is approximately 14 minutes in length. Please note that the interview shown on this DVD-ROM is a slightly extended version of the Speaking test. This allows for a wide range of language and types of response to be included. This interview also features high-level candidates whose performance would achieve a good pass in the exam. The video therefore provides a good model to follow. Don't worry if you feel you may not perform to this high standard in every area of the test. You will need to demonstrate a good level, but you will not need to use every structure or item of vocabulary perfectly in order to pass the test. Please see page 64 and pages 165–167 in the Practice Tests for the material used in this interview.

The video clearly details:

• the role of the examiners
• the timings of the test
• the four parts of the test and what is involved in each one.

Tips and advice

Following the Speaking test, there is a short clip to supplement the speaking tips given in the book. In this section, which is about five minutes long, an examiner gives some tips and advice about how to do well in the Cambridge English: First Speaking test.

The worksheet

This printable worksheet accompanies the complete Cambridge English: First Speaking test. Although primarily designed for self-study, the worksheet can also be used in the classroom. It provides in-depth information about the Speaking test and focuses on the language each candidate uses in the video.

The worksheet is divided into four sections, which relate to each part of the Speaking test. It includes activities which:

• draw students' attention to key features of the candidate's response
• relate these features to the marking criteria used by the examiners
• give the student practice in developing their own answers for similar questions.

A separate answer key and a full video script are also provided.